HOLY YES

A Collection of Poems, Prayers, and Lessons
for Living by Faith and Fulfillment in God

VICTORIA WASHINGTON

Holy Yes: A Collection of Poems, Prayers, and Lessons for Living by Faith and Fulfillment in God

For permission requests, write to the publisher at:
hello@iamvictoriawashington.com

ISBN: 979-8-218-63697-5

This is a collection of prayers, poems, and devotional reflections. The content is inspired by the author's personal faith, experiences, and creative expression. Any resemblance to actual persons, events, or places is either coincidental or intentionally used to honor the author's perspective and faith-based journey.

Cover Photo by Caroline Faulkinberry
Cover Design by Justine Mekler
Printed in the United States of America
First Edition: February 2025

To my beautiful sister, Veronica—

Your *Holy Yes* started it all.

You held Him in your heart far before I ever knew how. Because of your testimony, I have mine.

And together, we have ours. It's us for the Kingdom, *forever*.

I love you as deep as love goes.

———————————

And, to the King of Kings, Jesus.

Thank you for pursuing me, for saving my life, and giving me more than I could ever ask or imagine.

Table of Contents

How to Use This Book

Welcome to *Holy Yes*!

This book is designed to meet you wherever you are on your journey of faith and to ultimately, draw you closer to God's Word. Whether you're seeking daily inspiration, wrestling with challenges, or simply desiring a deeper connection with Scripture, this collection is a companion for your walk with Christ.

You can read it cover to cover, allowing each poem, prayer, reflection, and lesson to guide you through a cohesive narrative of surrender, renewal, and empowerment. You'll see the themes that come to life, echoing the timeless truths of the Bible: faith, perseverance, and courage.

Alternatively, you can use this book for individual moments of support, inspiration, encouragement, or connection. Simply open to a random page and trust that God will meet you there.

Most importantly, let this book be a bridge to God's Word.

Take time to reflect on the Scripture references and explore them further in your Bible. My prayer is that these pages deepen your understanding of God's promises and ignite a desire to immerse yourself in His Truth. Trust that every word is an *invitation*—to lean into God's presence, trust His plan, and grow in your faith.

Consider using this book in your quiet time with God in one of these ways:

- **As a Daily Devotional:** Begin each day with a poem or prayer that gently draws your heart into God's love and guidance, setting the tone for a day rooted in His presence.

- **Journaling Prompts:** Reflect on the lessons or questions stirred in you after reading, and let your thoughts flow freely onto the page.
- **Prayerful Contemplation:** Read a piece aloud during your prayer time, using it as a launching point to deepen your dialogue with God.
- **Business and Life Guidance:** Turn to its pages when you are facing decisions or challenges, letting the wisdom and encouragement within to help align your path with His Will.

Whether you spend five minutes or an hour within these pages, let this book be a sacred pause—a place to quiet your spirit, reconnect with God, and gather the strength to move forward with bold faith.

If you're new to walking with Christ, you'll find additional resources at the end of this book to support you on your journey.

I pray this book becomes a space where fear fades and you step confidently into a personal relationship with God through Jesus. May each piece remind you of His steadfast love, refresh your spirit, and equip you to declare your own *Holy Yes*.

A Special Message for New Believers

When I first returned to my relationship with God, I was so apprehensive about Christianity and wrestled with who Jesus is. I knew of Him as a 'character' in a story but never understood Him as Savior and Creator. This section is for believers who are new to walking with Christ or anyone who is reconciling with what the Gospel represents:

The Gospel

The word gospel means good news. At its core, the Gospel is the message of God's love and redemption for humanity. It declares that through Jesus Christ's life, death, and resurrection, we are offered forgiveness for our sins, reconciliation with God, and the gift of eternal life. The Gospel is an invitation to receive God's grace and live in the freedom of His truth.

Elaborating on The Gospel's Truth

Humanity was created in God's image, made to walk with Him in perfect relationship—free from sin and separation. As an act of love, God gave His creations free will, the ability to choose Him or turn away. This freedom was essential for genuine love and relationship to exist, for love cannot be forced—it must be chosen. However, when the first humans, Adam and Eve, used their free will to turn away from God, sin entered the world, breaking the intimacy they once shared with Him. And as descendants of Adam and Eve, sin entered humanity itself, becoming part of the world we are born into.

In the centuries that followed, the world was marked by sin, separation, and humanity's inability to reconcile with God on their own. Continuing to ignore God's guidance, humanity became lost—wandering in darkness, creating idols to fill the void, and seeking fulfillment in ways that only deepened the brokenness. Violence, greed, and selfishness became rampant, and the once-perfect relationship with God seemed like a distant memory.

Even then, God never stopped pursuing us. For thousands of years, He showed His love through prophets, signs, and promises of a Savior who would come to bring us back to Him.

That Savior is Jesus.

In an extraordinary act of love, God Himself came down as flesh, entering the world through the womb of a virgin. Jesus, fully God and fully human, came to reveal the heart of our Father and Creator. He walked among us, experiencing the joys and sorrows of life, yet remained without sin. He lived a perfect life, showing us how to love, pray, and walk in relationship with God.

Then, out of His great love, He took on the consequence for our sins on the cross. He died as the ultimate sacrifice, so we could be forgiven.

And the most beautiful part? The story doesn't end there.

On the third day, Jesus rose from the dead, defeating sin and death forever. His resurrection is the ultimate proof of His power and the promise of eternal life for all who believe in Him. Through His victory, a new covenant between God and humanity was born.

When you give your life to Christ, you are made new—a new creation *in* Him. By His death and resurrection, Jesus defeated the power of sin, and when you live in Him, sin no longer has power over you. Through His Spirit, you are empowered to walk in freedom and righteousness, no longer bound by the chains of the world.

The Gospel is the incredible news that Jesus opened the way for us to be restored to a relationship with God. Through faith in Him, we are forgiven, healed, and set free to live as God's beloved children. It's not about what we've done, but about what He's done for us.

When we say yes to Jesus, He fills us with His Spirit and gives us everything we need to have a perfect relationship with God—a gift that transforms us from the inside out.

This is the greatest love story of all time: the God of the universe coming to us fully human and fully divine and giving everything to bring us back to Him. His love is *unrelenting*, His grace is boundless, and His invitation is open.

The Trinity

The Trinity can be difficult to understand because it is beyond our human comprehension. However, once experienced, it simply ***clicks***. It would be impossible to write this book without referencing the Trinity so I want to break down how to metabolize it while you're reading this book.

The Trinity refers to the nature of God as one being expressed in three distinct persons:

- God, the Father
- God, the Son (Jesus)
- God, the Holy Spirit

C.S. Lewis provides one of the most powerful analogies I've come across, describing The Trinity as *The Three-Personal God*:

On a basic level, a straight line exists in one dimension. In two dimensions, those lines can come together in ways a one-dimensional world couldn't imagine, forming a square. In three dimensions, those squares can combine in even more unimaginable ways to create a cube. While each dimension builds upon the previous, the essence of the line, square, and cube remains connected. Similarly, the Trinity is one God expressed in three distinct and very real persons, each fully God yet intricately united.

This analogy reminds us that the complexity of God's nature is something we, as finite beings, may only begin to grasp. Just as a one-dimensional being could not comprehend a cube, we too are invited to marvel at the infinite depth of the God who created us, rather than limit Him to our understanding.

In our life in this natural world, we understand that one person is one being. I am me, and you are you. C.S. Lewis specifically writes, the Trinity describes a higher kind of life where you can have a being who is three Persons while remaining one Being, just as a cube is six squares while remaining one cube.

He goes on to explain that "Trinity-life" is there for us to experience: God (the Father) is the one we pray to, God (the Holy Spirit) is also the thing inside us urging us to pray, and God (the Son) is the bridge or road along which we are pushed towards God. It is, quite simply, *experiential.*

While they are distinct, together they are united in essence and purpose—showing us how God relates to us as Creator, Redeemer, and Sustainer. And ultimately, the Trinity leads us to having a personal relationship with our Creator.

The Holy Spirit

The Holy Spirit is God's presence *actively* at work in the world and within believers. He is our Counselor, Comforter, and Guide, who empowers us to live out our faith, understand Scripture, and grow in our relationship with God. Through the Holy Spirit, we experience God's transformative power in our lives.

Jesus is God

As God in human form, Jesus came to reveal His love, teach us Truth, and offer Himself as the perfect sacrifice for our sins. Throughout this book, you'll notice that Jesus is referred to as "He," emphasizing His humanity and divinity.

New Age Spirituality and Occult Practices

In this book, I also reference New Age Spirituality in contrast with the biblical teachings in this book, mostly because it's a huge part of my testimony and deliverance. New Age Spirituality is a broad movement that often focuses on self-help, channeling, and achieving higher states of God-like consciousness. It frequently includes practices like energy healing, astrology, mediumship, tarot and manifestation that is centered on human effort, source energy, multiple gods, and "The Universe" rather than reliance on the Creator of the universe (God).

While it may promise enlightenment or peace, in my experience and through my studies, New Age beliefs and practices directly distort or invert Biblical truths. This leads people away from the Gospel and further away from the real capital G, God. This book aims to equip believers with the tools necessary to discern between counterfeit healing and the life-giving Truth found in God's Word.

Sin and The Enemy

Throughout the book, you'll see several references to sin and the enemy. If you're coming from a New Age perspective that paints sin as an illusion or repression that needs to be "integrated to achieve wholeness" these terms might feel a bit jarring at first. I want to take a moment to break down what they truly mean.

Sin isn't about being shamed for doing something "bad." It's engaging in anything that separates us from God. Sin, very simply, means turning away from God and engaging in thoughts, actions, or activities that are outside of His original design for us.

Acknowledging sin doesn't mean living in fear. Instead, it means grounding ourselves in the Truth that God's love and power are infinitely greater than our sin. The more that we willingly give our hearts to God, the less we have a desire to sin.

You might wonder, "Why would God create sin and evil?" The answer is that God did not create sin or evil. God gave free-will to humanity and even heavenly beings. That means, we have the freedom to choose whether we will follow God or not. Evil and rebellion stems from the misuse of that free will. When humans deviate from God, sin is introduced to the world.

Later on in the book, I elaborate on what free will is and how it plays a role in having an intimate relationship with God but for now, I'll touch on one last piece:

God is good and without evil—1 John 1:5 reminds us: "God is light; in him there is no darkness at all." Evil is not a creation of God but rather a deviation from His goodness, a distortion introduced when free will is used to go against God's direction.

But the good news? Jesus. We have the Holy Spirit through Jesus who empowers us to overcome sin and resist the enemy. In Christ, we are no longer bound by the weight of evil or our own impulses. Instead, we are invited into a life of freedom, grace, and allegiance with God's Will. His sacrifice made a way for us to be reconciled to God once and for all, and the Holy Spirit prompts us on a daily basis to walk in truth, love, and victory every day

When I talk about sin and the enemy, it's not to invoke fear or shame but to point to the hope and redemption we have in Christ. We are not defined by our past or held captive by the lies of deception, but redeemed, renewed, and reconciled to God's original design.

God is my *how.*

Holy Yes: The Beginning of Everything

(My Testimony)

Summer of 2009.

I stared out the window as the lush green landscape turned into blurry brushstrokes.

No one knew I left.

It would take them a while to put the pieces together.

Probably as long as it took me to break them all apart.

Like a blanket that couldn't quite keep you warm at night, I rolled through the city half asleep and breathless.

Chicago had become a blended memory of clanking glasses over white lines of powder, rolling *I love-you's* in the 4am heat, and now, a *silent* goodbye.

The sky blushed at my morning smile, and the only reason I knew God existed was because I was still alive when I could have been dead.

I contemplated their faces, questions and shock as I drank my last six dollars in the form of dry red wine, in a plastic cup.

The familiar fog of relaxation rolled over my shoulders...

And there I was yet again, buzzed and breaking my own heart.

That was my favorite part about riding on trains.

Everything else seemed to be moving... *except* me.

Three years later, 2012.

The skyline looked like a tsunami-sized wave, as I pulled up to the toll booth.

She was covered in that same summer sun, each building teasing out a new memory from the riverbank of nostalgia.

I was back.

Returning to that same city, Chicago.

The one that held me in a chokehold, where it felt like walking on a tightrope, and all I could see was my past and present swimming underneath me.

It must be the athlete in me. I needed to win.

And leaving unannounced with dry wine on my lips felt like a loss I wasn't willing to take.

I had a college degree, a loving boyfriend, and a new job making $45,000 a year.

This time, it would be different. *Right?*

I stared straight ahead, hoping that if God did exist... somehow He would guide me.

One year later, 2013.

The tablet dissolved on the back of my tongue as the lights dimmed and neon flashes danced across my thighs.

In just a few moments, I would feel my heart expand and everything would soften like a rose opening underneath my thumb.

He was dancing in the middle of the restaurant, every move tugging at the corner of my mouth.

A man who made me smile just by being in the same room.

A man who *was* the love of my life.

I felt for the crystal around my neck, a clear quartz I wore for clarity and power as I was on a quest to become limitless.

As the ecstasy bloomed in my bloodstream, my index finger teased the edge of my wine glass, silently contemplating where I would pour myself into the evening.

Nights like these I became like a magnet.

Women flocked to me as I oozed with the confidence of a healer dressed in red. I would seemingly read their mind, and lock eyes with all the parts of them that felt small and unseen. I hugged and soothed their wounds, leaving them aghast at how I could untangle their whole story in one breath. Like a vampire drawing blood, I became addicted to their praise.

Men stared in admiration as I commanded the room, moving like an untouchable piece of gold. The wine stained ecstasy made its way to my feet. Like a jaguar slowly circling its prey, I stared back and took in the images they would draw on me with their eyes.

No one said a word.

No one knew I was faking it.

No one knew I was dead inside.

Night after night.

Weekend after weekend.

Chicago was my grave <u>and</u> my muse.

Until one afternoon... I felt the first knock.

A few months later.

My hands slapped across the white porcelain. Knees trembling under the cool tiles.

He wasn't home, and I was a master of secrecy.

I can't keep doing this, desperation raced across my mind.

I flushed last night's ecstasy and wine down the toilet, like clockwork.

I'd traded white lines for small pink tablets.

And there I was again, on a train moving without moving.

I looked around the room from the bathroom hallway. It was covered in altars that held various objects, crystals, grids, feathers, rattles, and angel cards.

On the outside, I was the most spiritual I'd ever been - teaching yoga, writing inspirational Facebook posts, and sharing picture-perfect images of my life.

Yet, I was the most lost I'd ever felt. Hiding addiction at the bottom of wine bottles, and escaping reality through EDM music and molly induced cuddle parties.

As I picked myself up off the bathroom floor, reality hit me. I wouldn't admit it at the time but I was a functioning alcoholic, who was unknowingly practicing witchcraft and self-idolatry, served up with a side of ecstasy.

The room went completely still as I lay on my bed, waiting for the painkillers to steal the ache from inside my chest.

With my eyes half closed, I drifted in and out of sleep.

And suddenly, as if there was a projector screen behind the lids of my eyes, I saw a calendar drawn over my life.

Am I hallucinating?

The vision zoomed all the way out and I could see above to the next dozen chapters of my life.

Through my hangover haze, words converted to English in my mind.

What is happening?

I heard: "By 30, you're going to get sober. You will not be drinking or doing any drugs in your 30's. You have until then."

An image of me with long hair and bright brown eyes raced to the front of my mind. (I had an afro at the time.)

That was in 5 years. I felt my heart whisper.

But I'm not an alcoholic. My mind fought back.

Who are you? My heart wondered.

I fell asleep, hugging the crystal around my neck.

It will all be better when I wake up, I thought to myself.

When I wake up.

Flash forward: Nine years later, 2022.

I woke up to anger burning inside my chest.

I was eight days sober and four years late.

But God was right on time.

The previous Sunday at Church, my pastor said we were doing a 40-Day Fast.

Each time I was at church, I didn't quite feel like I belonged, and secretly hoped I would be invisible while I figured out *why* I was there.

How could God still love me after all that I'd done? Is this real? Are these people really this happy?

In full transparency, I had no interest in religion or labeling myself a Christian. I didn't really understand Jesus or the Gospel.

But for some reason, each Sunday, I kept coming back.

My pastor said something that flew through the rows of pews to the back row, and straight into my heart.

"You can choose anything for your fast. Just remember, you aren't fasting from something... you're fasting for God to *search* you."

Immediately, I heard God say: you're giving up alcohol. The time is now.

As if someone's presence suddenly caught me by surprise, I sucked in a sharp breath of air.

Ouch. I'd given up ecstasy and 4am nights. I'd ended an engagement. I had left the city. I moved to California. I started my own business. I was making 7-figures. I had impact and influence.

But, I never broke the bottle.

The vision God showed me in my bedroom all those years ago slid forward. It felt like just yesterday I was laying backside, eyes half closed. The calendar. The warning. The next chapter. The woman with the long hair and bright eyes.

I was supposed to be completely sober by 30. I was 34.

On March 6th, 2022 I offered up one of the most important prayers of my life: "God, I cannot do this without you. But I am here. Search me for anything that isn't you... and remove it. I only want the real thing. *Please,* show me the real thing."

20 days into the fast.

I was halfway through the fast, yet no part of me felt anywhere close to sober.

Every part of me ached. And while I planned the exact red wine I would enjoy once the fast was over, I had somehow convinced myself that alcohol still had no power over me.

As I fasted, I journaled daily, listened to worship music on repeat, and continued to go to church on Sundays.

But, my heart was still closed.

The name Jesus felt threatening to me. I couldn't comprehend who He was or why we needed Him so much. But everyone seemed to love Him and had so many stories about how much He had helped them.

Out of nowhere, I was pulled to study Mary Magdalene's story. The woman Christ revealed Himself to after His resurrection. She was strengthened in Him, and I felt it through her love for Him. Through her testimony, I saw how Jesus saved and delivered her, through His ministry I saw how He taught her and loved her.

"I want to feel that...God show me how to feel that..." I thought.

I opened up the book I avoided for my whole life.

The Bible.

And I began reading God's Word. Where Jesus filled the pages from start to finish.

He is the voice that spoke light into existence in Genesis, the promise whispered to Abraham, the fulfillment of every prophecy, and the embodiment of God's love in the Gospels.

Every word, every story, pointed to Him—God's ultimate revelation wrapped in humanity. Jesus wasn't just a figure in the pages; He is the Word, alive, eternal, and breathing life into all who dared to believe. He is the Creator. He is Savior.

And just like that, God showed me the *real* thing.

My prayers began to change from begging to confidently requesting that Jesus purify my heart and renew my mind.

I stopped telling God what to do for me, and I began praising Him for the breakthrough I knew He was moving in me, through Christ.

Is Jesus real? Could He really heal me?

The End of The Fast: 40 days later.

For the first time as an adult, I went 40 days without a sip of alcohol.

I looked at myself in the mirror with a frame of light circling around it, and was in shock.

I wasn't thirsty.

I stared at my reflection: *Is this real?*

I stretched my tongue out and leaned towards the mirror to get a closer look.

I could not remember the taste of alcohol.

No, I mean it. I really couldn't remember the taste at all.

It was as if amnesia wiped out every memory of my favorite dry red wine.

I sifted through the tabs in my brain looking for the desire to pour a glass, to let the familiar buzz roll over me, to feel the power of ordering Veuve at a 5 Star Hotel at 12pm. I couldn't find it.

Where was the ritual of silent sips on evening walks, or the comfortably numb feeling I clung onto for years?

I *still* couldn't find it.

The shame.
The guilt.
The anxiety.
The back and forth.
The warfare.

It was gone.
In Jesus' name, it was finished.

I was in awe.

But, *now what?*

A few weeks later.

It became an undeniable truth in my heart: Jesus is real.

And He delivered me from addiction, shame, codependency... *darkness.*

Any craving to drink alcohol was wiped clean.

Yet, it was a well-kept secret that no one else knew.

This was just the beginning of my sanctification and walk with Christ.

It felt like a second chance at a life I didn't know what to do with.

I now believed in Jesus.

But I had yet to accept Him as my personal Lord and Savior. I had yet to give *my life.*

I was very public about my faith, going to church, and I often referenced God.

But, deep down, I was afraid to say His name... *Jesus.*

Less than six months later, July 2022.

It turns out Jesus will pursue you before you ever accept Him as savior.

My fast ended on April 15th.

By July, I was looking at:

A disintegrated business partnership.
Friendships ending that I thought would last a lifetime.
Ending a five year relationship.
Being single for the first time in ten years.
Moving up the coast on my own.

Anything and everything that God knew wouldn't bring me closer to Him was removed.

If this wasn't starting over, I don't know what is.

The Lord completely rearranged my life and set me apart to take me on the wildest adventure I'd ever go on.

And with nothing to lose and everything to gain in Him, there was only one thing left to say...

Holy Yes.

Two and a half years later–Today.

I am finishing the pages of this book from my condo in Los Angeles.

There's a cool breeze slipping through the sliding doors and a non-stop buzz from the city beneath me.

I look out at the horizon, overwhelmed by the sheer magnificence of God's love and unwavering plan.

I am the woman with bright brown eyes and long hair.

And I have never been more at peace in my entire life.

Exhale.

Your life *begins* with God's love.
Your life *continues* through God's glory.
Your life *renews* through God's restoration.

Faith will *boldly* move the first mountain.
Humility will *quietly* move the second mountain.

And through and through,
you are loved,
you are loved,
you are loved.

– *exhale.*

Faith

Your faith is the *ultimate* restoration.

It's the fertile soil that grows your belief into the behavior that displays God's character.

It's the riptide that keeps pulling you closer to Christ.

It's the part of you that trusts the sun to dip behind the mountains and beam through your morning window, day after day.

It's holding the bravery to walk without knowing, unwavering and committed.

It's moving with your eyes closed, *silently* trusting the space between where you are now and where God is moving you next.

It's relaxing into who you are in Him, and knowing *who* you belong to.

Faith doesn't come from the mind. It starts in the heart and grows through every cell, every ligament, every piece of tissue and bone in the body—until it becomes the very frame you exist within. When faith takes over the flesh, your testimony is born.

In walking with God, there are two types of faith: lukewarm faith and bone-deep faith.

Lukewarm faith is a faith that flutters on the surface, tethered to the flesh rather than rooted in the Holy Spirit. It's a half-hearted belief, where God's presence is *acknowledged* but not pursued. It's where faith becomes a box to check, a convenience rather than a commitment.

Lukewarm faith thrives on comfort—being content with just enough of God's presence to feel safe, but not enough to be *transformed*. It's the deception that we have everything we need within ourselves—that our human mind, our flesh, and our limited understanding are sufficient. Lukewarm faith whispers, "God is near, but I'll stay in control. I've got it figured out." Because deep down, you don't trust that God's way is better than your way.

Many walk around with lukewarm faith and they wonder why mountains don't move when they approach them. They wonder why they're insecure, uneasy, and constantly searching for clarity.

When you place more faith in the stars than you do in the One who created them, you're operating from lukewarm faith. When you find your identity through charts, keys, centers, and personality tests but have no idea who you are in God's eyes... you're settling for lukewarm faith.

In God's eyes, you are His beloved child (1 John 3:1), fearfully and wonderfully made (Psalm 139:14), and called for a purpose that only you can fulfill (Jeremiah 29:11). You are redeemed, forgiven, and seated in heavenly places with Christ (Ephesians 2:6). You are seen, known, and loved beyond measure.

Connecting to *that* identity? It requires bone-deep faith.

Bone-deep faith is faith that reshapes your very being. It penetrates beyond the surface, reaching the marrow of who you are. It's the kind of faith that doesn't just acknowledge God—it *clings* to Him.

Bone-deep faith surrenders the illusion of self-sufficiency, allowing God to reign in every corner of your life. It's faith that steps out of the boat, into the storm, and trusts that Jesus will hold you steady. Bone-deep faith leaves no room for lukewarm—it burns, it refines, and it transforms. This type of faith comes with responsibility. Because faith isn't a *feeling*—**it's an action. It's a choice.**

Bone-deep faith redirects your life. Those who have bone-deep faith have walked on fire (Daniel 9:25), they've stomped through the Red Sea (Exodus

14:21), they've followed wordless instructions through the wilderness (Exodus 13:21), and left everything behind without knowing what was next (Genesis 12:1).

Bone-deep faith doesn't just move the mountain—it gives you the sight to see *beyond* the mountain.

And that foundation is stronger than anything.

Now faith is confidence in what we hope for and assurance about what we do not see. This is what the ancients were commended for. By faith we understand that the universe was formed at God's command, so that what is seen was not made out of what was visible (Hebrews 11:1-3).

A faithful heart is one that is *completely* His.

Your Humanity

The burdens of the human soul become the beauty of the Holy Spirit when we surrender them to God. Yet surrender is no small thing. For many of us, it requires dismantling the pride and illusions we've clung onto tightly, for so long.

I used to believe that being right made me lovable. Pride wore me like a glove, convincing me that as long as I appeared infallible, I could hold on to love and approval. Wearing my self-righteousness like a badge of honor, I never wanted to be wrong. In arguments and disagreements, I fought to keep control, refusing to admit when I mishandled something or made a mistake. My pride wasn't just a flaw; it was a *fortress*—a barrier between me and the fullness of God.

There's a passage in the Bible that strikes me every time I read it:

"You show that you are a letter from Christ, the result of our ministry, written not with ink but with the Spirit of the living God, not on tablets of stone but on tablets of human hearts. Such confidence we have through Christ, before God" (2 Corinthians 3:1).

God writes His story on the human heart. Not on a perfect heart, not on a beautiful or polished heart, and not on a religious heart. On our **human** heart.

By ourselves, we are not enough (pride doesn't like to hear this). But the truth is, left to our own devices, our humanity is fragile, fractured, and flawed. But through Christ, our humanity is *redeemed*. It becomes the altar upon which God writes His greatest love story.

But first, we must **admit** we are human.

Then, we must **submit** our humanity to Christ.

And through Him, a new creation is born.

Admitting we are human is perhaps one of the hardest things we'll ever do. To acknowledge our humanness is to admit that we are limited, that our understanding is finite, and that we are not—and will *never* be—God.

But God, in His goodness, takes what is flawed and makes it complete and perfect *through* the gift of Jesus. He supplies grace for our limitations and uses our humanity as a canvas for His divinity.

> The more you surrender,
> the more God can work through you.
>
> The more God works through you,
> the more His vision is resurrected within you and the world.

You become the result of the Holy Spirit—an instrument for His power and truth.

When you admit to God that you are not enough on your own, you surrender to the fullness of His steadfast and abounding love.

> Will you keep carrying your burdens alone,
> or will you let God *transform* them into beauty
> beyond what you could ever ask or imagine?

"Now to him who is able to do immeasurably more than all we ask or imagine, according to his power that is at work within us" (Ephesians 3:20).

When you speak, imagine
you're using God's
paintbrush.

The paint is your heart,
and your words are the
brush.

If He is in your heart,
only His words can come
out of your mouth.

God Doesn't Need You Ready

To the one who has been spending her whole life getting ready...

You believed your readiness was needed to qualify you for the room.

Yet, where there is God, there is order.

There is a readiness that exists **before** you.

God is after your commitment, more than He is after your readiness.

Throughout the Bible, I noticed God never once asked His people... are you ready?

Instead, God *delivers* a promise.

God calls Abraham to leave his country, his family, and his father's house to go to a land He would show him. God doesn't give Abraham a map, a plan, or any proof of what's ahead—just a promise. Abraham commits and goes, not knowing where he is going.

Instead, God *offers* provision.

At the burning bush, God tells Moses to lead His people out of Egypt. Moses protests, saying he isn't eloquent and doesn't feel capable. God doesn't ask if Moses is ready. He assures him, "I will be with you," emphasizing God's provision over Moses' preparation.

Instead, God gives you a *position*.

Jesus reveals Himself to Peter and Andrew while they are fishing: "Follow Me, and I will make you fishers of men." He does the same with James and John. They immediately leave their nets and boats—without preparation or forewarning—and follow Him.

When you meet God's promise, provision and position with a *commitment...* your readiness is not required.

Very rarely will God reveal the full plan to the passenger.

Why?

Because unpredictability requires faith and dependency on Him. Not the plan.

So while you're waiting to feel ready, God is waiting for you to become loyal to Him, regardless of what the plan will be.

Commitment creates the loyalty and dedication necessary to depend on God, whether you are ready or not because you trust in who He is and you believe in all that He can do.

One of the most beautiful things about God's grace is that His plan goes *before* our circumstances. Meaning, whatever you are worried about, God has already moved ahead of it. This doesn't mean there won't be challenges, but He's established your steps to have authority in the face of any challenges that come up along the way. So it is written, the Lord Himself goes before you and will be with you; He will never leave you nor forsake you. Do not be afraid; do not be discouraged (Deuteronomy 31:8).

Yet, imagine God calls you...

And instead of *answering* His call with your commitment, you say "hang on, I gotta get ready."

But what are you getting ready for?

How could you possibly be ready for the Holy Mystery that is God's perfect plan?

The real question is: Are you willing to say Holy Yes *before* all the answers are laid out in front of you?

Your commitment says more about who you are than readiness ever will.

Because commitment has staying power that outlives *any* comfort zone.

When you have faith in God's plan, you move *no matter what*.

Turn overthinking into an overwhelming bout of trust in Him.

Turn worrying into pure wonder for all the ways He's going to move in this chapter of your life.

Remember that you were made by the Most High.

Remember who chose you.

And let this be a wake-up call.

Every time you think you need to "get ready" - imagine God is just outside the door waiting for you... and instead of asking a question, you answer with the *decision* to step forward.

God is Not a Spiritual Concept

God is the Creator (the, meaning singular).

A concept is an abstract idea; a general notion. When you hold God as a concept in your head, it places Him as a theory in your life versus the Truth of your life. In that, you risk making Him fit into your ideas versus you committing to His Will.

"All things were created through him, and apart from him not one thing was created that has been created" (John 1:3).

God is Christ.

Knowing Jesus is knowing God Himself. Christ is not just a teacher or prophet, but God *incarnate*—living, real, and full of grace and Truth. As Megan Fate Marshman so beautifully spoke in one of her sermons, "our God knew that you could not climb up the ladder to be with Him so He climbed down the ladder to be with us. Every other world religion says try harder. Christianity says, receive it more. Let Him love you. Let Him be near to you."

"Jesus told him, 'I am the way, the truth, and the life. No one comes to the Father except through me. If you know me, you will also know my Father. From now on, you do know him and have seen him'" (John 14:6-7).

God is the Spirit.

The Holy Spirit is intimately connected with Jesus and the Father, speaking only what He hears from God. The Spirit is not separate from God, but the very presence and voice of God working *within* us.

"When the Spirit of truth comes, He will guide you into all the truth. For He will not speak on His own, but He will speak whatever He hears. He will also declare to you what is to come. He will glorify Me, because He will take from what is Mine and declare it to you" (John 16:13-14).

God is the house.

Jesus is the doorway. The Holy Spirit is the furniture that fills the space.

Without God, there is nothing—no house, no foundation, no creation.

Without Jesus, the doorway to intimacy with God is compromised. It leaves us unable to fully experience the depth of connection and the perfect relationship with God that we were created for.

Without the Holy Spirit, the house remains quiet and unfilled. It's missing the guidance, comfort, and voice that shapes and transforms us along the way.

How brilliant is it that God's omnipresence creates a trinity of Truth? To comprehend this with the logical brain is impossible, but to feel the supernatural shift in your heart is a gift.

Together, the Trinity gives us the fullness of God's presence: a firm foundation in the Father, a clear pathway to intimacy through Jesus, and the Holy Spirit who resides within us, filling our lives with guidance and transformation.

Everything we'll ever need, made in the image of one Holy being.

You can continue to ask the universe for "signs."

You can "trust the universe" to attune you and let the universe develop your character...

<u>Or</u> you could turn towards God, who created the universe.

The first step in building intimacy and a true relationship with God, is to stop replacing the creator with a creation.

The More We Depend on God

God measures our success not by worldly achievements, but by our dependence on Him. "Not by might nor by power, but by my Spirit,' says the Lord Almighty" (Zechariah 4:6).

The more we depend on God, the more successful we are, because we are filled with our ultimate purpose: to know Him and make Him known. "Seek first the kingdom of God and His righteousness, and all these things will be added to you" (Matthew 6:33).

The more that you depend on God, the more you are sustained by His unfailing love and resources. As you pray for God to scale your life, don't forget to also pray that He scales your dependence on Him. This allows "His strength to be made perfect in your weakness" (2 Corinthians 12:9).

In today's society, dependence is often viewed as weakness, especially among women. We're told to be self-made, self-reliant, and independent at all costs. But this mindset keeps us striving and disconnected from the only source that truly *sustains* us—Jesus.

Through Christ, dependence is transformed into a beautiful life of healing, restoration, and strength. It's in letting go of the illusion of control that we step into the freedom of our new nature in Him. "Therefore, if anyone is in Christ, the new creation has come: The old has gone, the new is here!" (2 Corinthians 5:17).

As your intimacy with God deepens, you discover that dependence on Him isn't a burden that takes from you—it's a gift that fills and sustains you.

This dependence gives you the vision, the resourcefulness, the creativity, the strength, and the ideas to move forward regardless of your circumstance. It shifts your perspective from striving to abiding, aligning your life with His will and provision.

When your desire shifts from wanting to be seen and known in the world to "I want to be known by the One who created me," you will move differently. Your actions will flow from the confidence of *already* being fully loved and chosen. There's no need to prove yourself, at all. "For we are God's masterpiece. He has created us anew in Christ Jesus, so we can do the good things He planned for us long ago" (Ephesians 2:10).

You are successful upon arrival. You are overflowing and completely filled, not because of what you have achieved, but because of who you are in Christ.

Miracle

"But if I were you, I would appeal to God; I would lay my cause before Him. He performs wonders that cannot be fathomed, miracles that cannot be counted."
(Job 5:8-9)

A prayer becomes a miracle the moment you realize you can't do it without God intervening. That's on purpose, rather than an accident or coincidence.

When you look up the definition of miracle, it says a miracle is an extraordinary event that *comes with* divine intervention in human affairs. You will not see God deliver a miracle without first changing and intervening with what is.

Miracles happen by faith *through* change. That means, you can't receive a miracle without also receiving change.

And so if you're afraid of change, you're also afraid of miracles.

In the New Testament, the Gospels record 37 miracles of Jesus and they all have one thing in common:

> They reveal the *outstanding* nature of God,
> where He intervened in our human affairs.

Jesus turned water into wine, fed thousands from one loaf of bread, straightened backs, healed blind eyes, and calmed storms. Each of these miracles required an internal shift within the people involved—a willingness to surrender their logic, doubts, and control to the power of God.

When Jesus turned water into wine, it wasn't just about the wine; it required the servants to **trust His instruction** to fill jars with water, even when it made no sense (John 2:1-11). Feeding thousands called the disciples to **relinquish their scarcity**, offering the little they had with faith that God's provision would be more than enough (John 6:1-13).

Straightening backs and healing blind eyes demanded the recipients to **confront their hopelessness and take bold steps of faith**, trusting Jesus' power to restore what seemed impossible (Luke 13:10-17; Mark 10:46-52). Even calming storms forced the disciples to **confront their fear** and realize their need to trust fully in Jesus' authority over all creation (Mark 4:35-41).

In each instance, the miracle didn't just change circumstances; it changed hearts, deepened faith, and revealed God's glory in a profound and personal way.

Again, you cannot pray for a miracle without also praying for *change*.

Instead of, *"God, I need this miracle. Please bring me this. I will do whatever you ask me to do."*

Your prayer becomes, *"You are the God of miracles, Lord. I trust you. In You, I hold the courage to confront my fear. Use this moment for Your Glory. I surrender my logic and my doubt, and I pick up Your courage and Your confidence. Be with me, as I confront scarcity and take a bold step of faith. Guide me Holy Spirit, to be who God calls me to be. I am willing to change. I am willing to shift. Show me what I need to see and let go of. Renew my mind and make my life a display of your miraculous grace. Thank you. In Jesus' mighty and majestic name, I offer this prayer. Amen."*

God has many miracles for you. But first, you will need to relinquish something. You will be called to confront something. You will be asked to trust, even when it makes no sense. Because as much as God is performing the miracle, He's using your body, your mind, and your heart to do it, so it all has to be *surrendered* to Him.

Mary, the mother of Jesus, exemplifies this so powerfully. When the angel Gabriel announced that she would carry the Son of God, it was not the miracle Mary had imagined for her life. It disrupted her plans, placed her in a vulnerable position, and called her to walk a path of immense faith and courage. Yet, she responded with surrender: *"I am the Lord's servant. May your word to me be fulfilled."* (Luke 1:38)

Mary carried the miracle of Jesus not just in her *body*, but in her *obedience*, her endurance, and her willingness to trust God's plan even when it defied logic and invited misunderstanding. Her story reminds us that miracles often come with *weight*—but it is the weight of God's glory working through us.

When you pray for a miracle, know you are praying to make your life an example of His Word. There's responsibility and reverence that comes with *carrying* a miracle through. Instead of feeling the weight of your circumstances, feel the weight of God's promise. And then when the miracle occurs, it will call you into a new way of life. It will change *everything* in you.

And oftentimes, how the miracle unfolds will be in a deeply unexpected way because the miracle is not what you told God you need... the miracle is what God knows is best for you. So, don't let your entitlement for what you think God *owes you* distract you from being open and receptive to what God offers you for your evolution.

The most beautiful part?

Each time God moves a miracle through, He creates *evidence* for the unbeliever and a *revelation* for the believer. That means, while you're praying for a miracle, someone else is praying for theirs, and when your miracle arrives, it will provide evidence for someone else.

A miracle is more than an answer to your prayer; it is an invitation to step into God's plan for your life. It's not just about receiving—it's about *becoming*. Becoming someone who trusts Him beyond understanding, someone who surrenders fear and control, and allows their life to reflect His power and glory.

Miracles don't just change your circumstances; they transform your heart, deepen your faith, and position you to be a vessel for His Kingdom.

So when you pray for a miracle, be committed.

31

Be committed to let go, to be reshaped, and to rise into the version of yourself that God envisioned from the very beginning of your existence. Because when the miracle comes, it won't just bless you—it will ripple out into the lives of others, bearing witness to His love, His power, and His unending grace.

That's the miracle within the miracle: it's never just about you. It's about God's Kingdom coming alive in your body, through you, and for the world to see.

Miracle Prayer

God,

I come to You with an open and humble heart. You are the redeemer. You are the miracle worker. Excavate, dissolve, remove anything that isn't You. I am open to change, across any area of my life that You know needs it.

Your miracles deliver, they interrupt, and they transform. I believe in You, I place my hope in You, and I fix my gaze on You.

You are my maker and I am Your daughter before anything.

Father God, I lean into You for peace and reconciliation. For joy, for hope, and for creativity.

Hold me in this change. Teach me to accept the shifts in this season and to fully surrender into Your grace.

In Jesus' name,

Amen

Reclaiming Your Imagination for God's Glory

I used to think imagination was a function of the mind. But I've come to know it as a *mirror*—a reflection of the heart. It's the space between soul and spirit, the wellspring of life, where the invisible becomes visible. It's where God delivers His vision along with new ideas, wisdom, and desires.

The imagination is powerful. It can present itself as reality through sensations, feelings, and emotions, altering what you see, think, and believe. When healthy, the imagination becomes fertile ground for God's greatness to take root. It is ripe with a yearning soil where His vision can grow.

But when unhealthy, the imagination becomes a breeding ground for the enemy to plant seeds of ingratitude and unbelief. We become plagued by worry, guilt, and anxiety, losing sight of the beauty, truth, and goodness of God. This makes the imagination one of our most valuable and sensitive forms of communication with God.

While God uses your imagination to deliver the divine, the enemy seeks to distort it. The devil doesn't go after your mind; he goes after your imagination first. Because if he can corrupt your imagination, he can reach your heart.

And once he's infiltrated your heart, he can present falsehoods as reality, pulling you away from God's truth. Jesus warns in Matthew 15:18-19, "But the things that come out of a person's mouth come from the heart, and these defile them. For out of the heart come evil thoughts—murder, adultery, sexual immorality, theft, false testimony, slander." What starts in your imagination, makes its way to your heart, and then comes out of your mouth. It becomes the very thing you see and believe.

Without a solid anchor in God, it's easy to mistake these falsehoods for truth. You might even be wondering, "but how do I know I'm hearing God's voice, and not my voice or the enemy's?"

Remember: the more time you spend in God's Word, the more you learn how He speaks, gives direction, and guides His people. The more you learn how He sounds, loves, and corrects, the more you'll be able to easily identify if something comes from Him.

If you hear something and you can't trace it back to God's Word (The Bible), it simply didn't come from Him. For example, if I hear *"you should be ashamed of yourself"* or *"you're never going to get them to understand you"* or *"don't eat that, you'll be fat"* – I know that's not from God because that's not how God speaks or leads His people.

God says:

- *"There is therefore now no condemnation for those who are in Christ Jesus"* (Romans 8:1).
- *"The Lord is my helper; I will not be afraid. What can man do to me?"* (Hebrews 13:6).
- *"For I know the plans I have for you," declares the Lord, "plans to prosper you and not to harm you, plans to give you hope and a future"* (Jeremiah 29:11).

The enemy accuses and condemns. God corrects, comforts, and reassures.

Often, we grow impatient waiting for God to deliver an answer or to fulfill His vision, so we create our own answer or turn to other sources like psychics, mediums, tarot, or astrology to determine our next steps. These sources promise quick clarity, and the enemy uses them to prey on our desire for speed and control. Satan knows humanity is addicted to instant gratification, and he'll leverage that addiction to present counterfeit answers that appear satisfying on the surface, but lead us further from God's plan.

When we act on these counterfeit answers, we risk stepping outside of God's Will and create situations God never asked us to walk into. Our impatience can lead us to build plans, make decisions, or pursue relationships that lack the foundation and protection of His guidance. An answer or a vision born outside of God is *hollow*—it may offer temporary relief, but it lacks the depth, clarity, and peace that can only come from Him.

God's timing often requires *patience* because He's preparing us for what He's planned, ensuring it aligns with His purpose. When we rush ahead, we settle for less and that settling carries consequences. True trust in God means learning to endure tension and discomfort, knowing that His answers are *always* worth the wait.

This is why we must heal our imagination. The imagination is the space where God's vision takes root in your heart. When the enemy steals your imagination, he's attempting to disrupt the delivery of God's vision. A lack of imagination creates a lack of perception—your intelligence, your wealth, your identity, and your ability to bring things into form.

When you root your imagination in God, it becomes a sacred space where His vision flourishes. It's a place of divine creativity, where the impossible becomes possible and your faith is made visible.

Your imagination is designed to be used as a wellspring for His Glory.

In this moment, *declare* that you are taking your imagination back.

Speak these words aloud:

In Jesus' name, I declare no weapon formed against me shall prosper.

I take back my imagination and place it under the authority of Christ.

God, renew my heart and cleanse my mind,
so that my imagination becomes a vessel for Your vision.

My thoughts align with Your truth,
and my beliefs are anchored in Your promises.

Guard my heart from the enemy's lies,
and fill my imagination with Your wisdom, creativity, and divine purpose.

Thank You, Lord, for the gift of imagination
—a space to receive Your vision and bring forth Your glory.

I surrender this space to You completely,
trusting in Your guidance and provision.

In Jesus' name,

Amen

Being Known by God

It's one thing to know God. It's another thing entirely to house the feeling of being *known* by God.

The difference is like opening a window after sitting in a room filled with stale air. Suddenly, a rush of fresh air fills the space, awakening your senses and making you aware of everything you'd been missing. Everything feels alive, intentional, and connected.

The more your relationship with God through Christ deepens, the more revelation you are able to receive.

You may be asking, "why *through* Christ?"

Jesus is God in the flesh. Before Jesus, we had to go through prophets, priests and sacrifices. But after Him, the veil was broken and we were given direct access to God, our Heavenly Father. When we know Jesus, we have everything we need to have a *personal* relationship with Our Creator, God.

The truth is:

Revelation is God *revealing* direction to you.

Revelation doesn't strike; it *reveals*. To reveal is to make something previously unknown, known. It's allowing something unseen to come into focus through supernatural means.

We often expect or hope for God to appear out of thin air, like a lightning bolt cutting through the sky. But revelation isn't theatrical—it's *relational*.

In New Age practices through different ceremonies and rituals, I used to receive "big downloads" from various gods, angels, and entities, believing it was God speaking to me.

I later learned these experiences were counterfeits of God's true revelation. They were loud, frenzied, and theatrical, designed to distract me from the still, small voice of the Lord (1 Kings 19:12). Scripture warns us of false gods and deceptive spirits that come clothed in charisma, drawing people away from the truth. "For such men are false apostles, deceitful workers, masquerading as apostles of Christ" (2 Corinthians 11:13).

God isn't waiting to make Himself known through spectacle; He's in the room right now, ready to meet us where we are.

Are you ready to *listen*?

Too often, we're desperate for God to hear us, but forget to listen so we can hear Him first. I'm reminded of the scripture: "So then faith comes by hearing, and hearing by the word of God" (Romans 10:17).

This means faith doesn't just come from speaking; it comes from listening— to the Word, not the world. If you have *faith* in God's Word, you will *hear* God's Word. If you have faith in the world or false gods, you will hear from false gods and have a harder time distinguishing between what is God's voice and everything else.

Ultimately, listening leads to obedience. And in obedience, God unveils what was hidden. He opens our eyes to see what we couldn't before. But revelation doesn't come on our schedule; it comes on God's timing. He has a time for everything and a way that is unmatched.

And when He does give you direction, even if it doesn't make sense, don't hesitate. Buy the ticket. Take the ride. God's plan always exceeds our understanding.

I pray that you experience a *revelation*–one that stems from your personal relationship with the One true God. I pray He reveals Himself in a way only He can, and that you turn toward His Word with faith and bravery in your heart. Through your listening, I pray you hear. May you hear everything He has for you and may you know, deep in your soul, the One it came from.

Being known by God is a process, not a default. It requires us to position our hearts intentionally towards Him. When we surrender our thoughts, feelings, character, behaviors, and even the way we walk and talk to God, He begins to shape us under His covenant. This isn't passive; it's a commitment to say, "I want to be known by God."

When that becomes your focus, *everything shifts*.

Our problem is not that God is taking too long to reveal the plan for our life.

It's that we're begging Him to move us more than we're praying for Him to *purify* us.

Revelation follows purification.

So I hold on to scripture,
Your Word like a dove,
planted inside my chest.
Do not be afraid, You say.
I place both feet on the ground.
To walk with You is like flying,
with the world upside down.

– *surrender.*

morning prayer.

God,

I allow You into my heart.
I allow You into my mind.
I allow You into my sight.

Today, may I be moved as Your vessel.
I am Your canvas to create through.

Lord, I know You make the darkness tremble.
And where there is division and deception,
may Your light enter as the *sword of Truth*.

Take my desires and turn them
into what You want for me, Lord.

I receive Your Holy Spirit,
as the *empowerment* of my life.

May I know today, as You would have me see it.

Thank you. Thank you. Thank you.

In Jesus' Mighty and Majestic Name I pray,

Amen

What No One Tells You About Prayer

Prayer is more about you giving to God, than God giving to you.

You're giving your time. Your trust. Your thoughts. Your words. Your fears. Your hopes. Your dreams. Your beliefs. Your life.

And you're not giving it to an imaginary concept in the sky. You're giving it to the One who has *given* life to you.

Prayer is a unique expression of your dependency on God.

"In the days of his flesh, Jesus offered up prayers and supplications, with loud cries and tears, to him who was able to save him from death, and he was heard because of his reverence" (Hebrews 5:7).

This verse shows us something profound: prayer, at its root, is an offering. Jesus *offered up* His prayers; He didn't demand answers or pull them down as if they were owed to Him. To offer something is to approach with humility, to surrender it willingly into the hands of another.

Imagine holding something precious in your hands—a delicate vase, a treasured heirloom. You lift it up, fully aware of its value, and place it into the care of someone you trust, knowing they will handle it with the greatest tenderness and wisdom. That's what it means to offer up a prayer to God. It's a surrender of our burdens, desires, and fears into the hands of the only One who is able to carry them.

When we pray as an offering, we're not trying to control the outcome. Instead, we release our prayers as an *act of reverence*, trusting that God will do what is good, right, and best. It's not a transaction; it's an acknowledgment that He alone is able.

"And he was heard because of his reverence" (Hebrews 5:7).

Later in the verse above we see, Jesus' prayers were heard *because* of His reverence and submission. This is a powerful reminder that God values a humble and surrendered heart, more than a list of desires, accomplishments, or perfection.

Jesus taught, "When you pray, do not be like the hypocrites, for they love to pray standing in the synagogues and on the street corners to be seen by others" (Matthew 6:5).

Prayer is not performance or something to tick off your to-do list. It's not a drive-thru station where you order your requested meal of the day. And it's definitely not a habit or ritual to appear more spiritual or pious.

Instead, Jesus says, "When you pray, go into your room, close the door, and pray to your Father, who is unseen" (Matthew 6:6). This reveals God's preferred location for prayer: a private moment for you to come together with Him as your Heavenly Father. Here, Jesus also instructs us on **who** to pray *to*. This means **who** we pray to is more important than *what we pray for*.

"Then your Father, who sees what is done in secret, will reward you. And when you pray, do not keep on babbling like pagans, for they think they will be heard because of their many words" (Matthew 6:7).

God prefers quality over quantity. He doesn't need clever words or overly-rehearsed thoughts that sound like poetry. Your humanness is the perfect ingredient for His divinity to shine through. Remember, you coming to God unfinished becomes His greatest masterpiece, every time. And it's important to note, reward is not a special prize that only the "good little girls" get. Reward at its root means to be recognized. To be rewarded by God is to be recognized by Him.

The sweetest surprise happens next when Jesus says: "Do not be like them, for your Father knows what you need *before* you ask Him." This is part of the gift of being known by God–you were His idea, so He knows exactly what you need at the exact time–even if it doesn't seem like it.

Prayer is not about getting all of your desires met or telling God what you want—it's an act of listening so you can hear what He *already* has for you. In prayer, God reveals plans, visions, and next steps to an obedient heart prepared to follow and ears ready to listen.

God knows what is essential to your growth. And in prayer, you begin to understand the ways He's preparing to nourish and sustain you through every phase of your life.

When your prayer shifts from *listing* all the things you want to *listening* for all that He wants to bestow within you, then your personal relationship with God deepens. And if you arrive to pray knowing that God is *for* you, it relieves you of begging and prepares you for becoming.

You no longer have to figure out how to get what you want because you can simply linger in His presence and grace.

And in that, you have *everything*.

Sometimes God's voice is
so simple that it will make
you weep;

the simplicity is a reprieve
for the soul, in a world
that can feel remarkably
complicated.

Why Obedience is the Greatest Act of Love

Our free will is a gift that often goes overlooked in conversations with God. It signifies the profound truth that we have a choice. This freedom isn't accidental—it was intentionally designed to activate our trust in God's Will. Far from being a coincidence, our ability to choose lies at the heart of the covenant between us and God.

God gave us the gift of choice because love, trust, and faith cannot exist without it.

As C.S. Lewis beautifully wrote:

"If a thing is free to be good it is also free to be bad. And free will is what has made evil possible. Why, then, did God give them free will? Because free will, though it makes evil possible, is also the only thing that makes possible any love or goodness or joy worth having. A world of automata--of creatures that worked like machines--would hardly be worth creating. The happiness which God designs for His higher creatures is the happiness of being freely, voluntarily united to Him."

If we were programmed to automatically follow God's Will, our relationship with Him would be robotic and obligatory, not rooted in love and trust. By giving us free will, God invites us to actively choose Him, showing that our decision-making holds weight in His eternal plan.

When you're choosing between free will and God's Will, oftentimes, you're choosing between eternal life or fleeting pleasures. It is through this lens that free will transforms from a mere ability to get what we want into a ripe opportunity to grow more intimate with our Creator.

But here's where it gets challenging: choice also requires obedience, and obedience often starts with submission. The struggle to be obedient usually stems from the struggle to submit. Before we can submit, we must admit.

Admit that we need God.

This is where resistance often arises. Maybe you've submitted to authority before, and ended up getting hurt. Maybe you've admitted you needed someone, and they didn't show up. These experiences can create a barrier in our hearts, making us hesitant to fully trust God, even though His authority is perfect and His love never fails.

So what does obedience truly mean, beyond the pain we may project onto it? Obedience in its most authentic form means 'in accordance with' or 'submission to another's authority.' But the beautiful thing is this: God holds authority and also gives us free will. He doesn't force us to abide—He invites us to.

When I struggle with obedience, I remind myself: I am God's idea, not my own. He knows better than me, and the sooner I admit that, the sooner I will submit to His direction *and* His ways.

God is loving, *yes* and that doesn't mean He won't ask you to walk away before you're ready, or let go of something you currently enjoy. Because not everything that you enjoy is good for you. Not everything *you* want is an experience God wants for you. You might want a specific version of "success," but success isn't what *you* do, it's being obedient to what God wants to do through you.

Scripture reminds us, 'I have the right to do anything,' you say—but not everything is beneficial. 'I have the right to do anything'—but not everything is constructive." (1 Corinthians 10:23)

This reminds us that just because we desire or enjoy something doesn't mean it is good for us in the context of God's plans.

While you have free will to choose if you'll follow Him or not, God is sovereign and ultimately decides what is best for humanity. Similar to a parent and child—the mother gives birth to the daughter, and while the daughter can choose whether she will listen or not, ultimately, the mother decides: *TV is not healthy for you in the morning, so we're not turning it on.*

The daughter, who really wants to watch TV, becomes upset. She doesn't understand why something she enjoys is being withheld from her.

But the mother sees what the daughter cannot—how starting the day glued to the screen might make her restless, distracted, or unprepared for school. The mother envisions the bigger picture: her daughter growing up healthy and vital, forming habits that serve her well in the future. The daughter may not understand the reasoning now, but the mother's decision is rooted in love, even if it feels restrictive in the moment.

In the same way, God, as our Heavenly Father, sees beyond the temporary satisfaction of our desires. He lovingly withholds or redirects us, not to punish or frustrate us, but to align us with a greater path that we often can't see. Just as the child must learn to trust her parent's wisdom, so must we learn to trust God's wisdom, even when His ways challenge our wants.

As the older sibling who grew up way too fast and someone who identifies as a leader, I'll be the first to admit I had a huge problem with this. I thought God's commands were just a bunch of rules designed to keep people from enjoying life. They felt like restrictions, not protection. And as for the Bible? I didn't think it held any real weight. To me, it was just an outdated book written by a bunch of random people a long time ago—irrelevant to my life and out of touch with the world I lived in so I honestly never took the time to read it.

But then God, in His infinite patience, began to open my eyes. It wasn't through a loud, dramatic moment but through quiet nudges and experiences that softened my resistance. I started to notice how empty my own plans left me, no matter how much I tried to lead myself. The decisions I thought were so freeing often led to frustration and confusion. Slowly, I began to realize that my version of freedom wasn't freedom at all—it was a cycle of chasing what felt good in the moment and ending up with more questions than answers.

That's when I started to approach the Bible differently. Instead of seeing it as a rigid set of ancient rules, I began to see it as alive, dynamic, and deeply personal. I saw how its words spoke directly to the struggles I thought were too modern or unique to be addressed. I realized that the Bible wasn't just written by man—it was inspired by God Himself, breathed out as a guide to help me navigate not only my choices but my very identity. It became clear that His commands weren't there to stifle me but to lead me into the *fullness* of life He had designed for me.

The more I leaned in, the more I saw the Bible as a living, breathing word—timeless in its truth and always relevant to my heart. It became a place where I could hear God's voice, experience His love, and find clarity for the moments when life felt overwhelming. I didn't just start reading it; I started *listening*, trusting, and letting it shape me. And in doing so, I realized that God wasn't trying to control me—He was inviting me to be free in ways I didn't even know were possible.

And here's the best part: I didn't have to figure it all out on my own. Through Christ and in the Holy Spirit, my heart changed in ways I never thought possible. My resistance to God—my pride and sense of self-sufficiency—started to melt away, replaced by a growing reverence for Him. It wasn't that I suddenly became perfect or had all the answers, but the struggle to follow Him turned into a desire to honor Him. Not because I felt obligated, but because I had experienced His love so deeply that I wanted to respond in that same love.

If you're looking for a place to start, begin by admitting:

God, I need You, and I feel resistant at times.
Help me to live in accordance with Your Will.
Help me to know You intimately and completely.
I choose to turn towards You.
You made me and know what's next.
Holy Spirit, soften my heart.
May Your love swallow any fear,
As I walk boldly in my faithfulness.

In Jesus' name I pray,

Amen

Suddenly, obedience becomes a choice, and that choice becomes the greatest act of love between you and your Creator.

If you're going
to chase anyone,
chase Jesus.

When Who You Were No Longer Fits Who You've Become

Following God is like living on the edge of a memory.

Every step is a paper thin line between the old self you were once attached to and the new you that He redeemed. Things you used to love, no longer hold the same luster.

You look around the room and it's like God turned the lights on and everyone who once wore a costume has now been exposed; the people you admired aren't so appealing anymore. The clothes you used to wear no longer fit who God molded and sculpted in His image.

Your desires are now like an old bookshelf. You revisit that shelf from time to time, trying to find that book you loved, and remember that one line in chapter 5 you once adored. And then you realize those stories aren't useful anymore. It's now His desires that live within you. They're different from what you would choose. Yet, they feel more fulfilling than you could ever imagine.

You have been crucified with Christ, and you no longer live, but Christ lives in you. The life you now live in the body, you live by faith in the Son of God, who loved you and gave himself for you (Galatians 2:20).

This world now feels oddly unfamiliar. It's like you're on a road trip to an unknown destination, and you're pausing at a rest stop to gain your bearings. All the roads you used to know by heart, have been replaced with new gravel that's never been traveled on. You're searching for the keys in your purse... shaking out the dust from old receipts. You find that note you wrote with your favorite pen years back, caught up in the nostalgia, only to realize you don't have the keys.

You don't have the keys.

God holds the door open to the backseat for you, the one right behind the driver. You're reminded that all roads lead to Him, so there's no need for a map, keys, or an endless search for a destination.

He is the destination. You have arrived.

Every day becomes a mark of glory as He wins your soul and snatches you from darkness. Every breath lives as a testimony to His grace and perfect plan. The drive isn't always smooth, but there's something soothing about riding with the King of Kings. The one who built the road in the first place. The God who makes all things good, even the impossible parts that feel staged by the devil himself.

A deep and unshakeable trust begins to form as God drives. You take in the view from His perspective, seeing all the parts you missed when you were too concerned with it being *your way*.

An exhale escapes your lips just past the bend... and for the first time, maybe in your whole life, you relax. Your spine hugs the leather seat and you roll the window down to drink in the wind of peace. It quenches every thirst, as Jesus reminds you from the passenger seat: "but whoever drinks from the water that I will give him will never get thirsty again. In fact, the water I will give him will become a well of water springing up in him for eternal life" (John 4:13-14).

God shows you the backway to your dreams, and there's a new, off-road confidence assembling at your feet. Shame burns under the tires as you gaze across the valley floor. Just like God's Word says, "Look, I have given you the authority to trample on snakes and scorpions and over all the power of the enemy; nothing at all will harm you" (Luke 10:19).

Now, each step you take has been established and chosen. There's an authority in the way you move; a humble gaze as you walk, knowing deep down this authority is not a product of your own doing. It is a gift to behold.

And even though you aren't always going to feel like doing what God asks you to do - wisdom carries you to "trust in the Lord with all your heart and lean not on your own understanding" (Proverbs 3:5).

Following God is like cliff diving into eternity, "for whoever sows to please the Spirit, from the Spirit will reap eternal life" (Galatians 6:8).

Where God is, everything is possible. He calls you to remember that in His Son, Jesus, He created The Way. The Truth. The Life.

You smile into the rearview mirror, another exhale moves through your body.

The road stretches ahead, endless and full of mystery. But now, it no longer terrifies you. Instead, it invites you. The landscape of your life, once blurry with uncertainty, begins to sharpen with divine clarity. The trees along the way whisper His promises, their branches bending gently to form a canopy of grace over your journey.

And as you ride, something profound settles in your spirit—you're no longer chasing something. You're being *carried*. Carried by the One who knows the bends, the valleys, and the mountaintops before you ever take a breath to notice them.

In the distance, the horizon glows—not with the fading light of this world, but with the brilliance of God's eternal presence. You realize this isn't just a road; it's a pilgrimage, a holy journey back to the heart of the Father.

The past, once a burden, has become evidence that God is real. Every misstep redeemed, every scar a signpost of His mercy.

And as the car hums along, the rhythm of God's heartbeat becomes your own. His desires, His vision, His plan—no longer foreign, but familiar, like a melody you've known all along but are just now remembering.

The rearview mirror reflects a glimpse of who you used to be—a reminder, not a regret. That version of you paved the way for this moment, where everything becomes new. The version of you who said *Holy Yes*.

The journey isn't about arriving anymore; it's about abiding. Abiding in the presence of the King who doesn't just guide the way but *is* the way. You smile, not because the road is easy, but because the road is good. And in this silent surrender, you find freedom.

This is what it means to follow God—to cliff-dive into eternity, knowing that the fall isn't the end, but the beginning of everlasting life.

No relationship will call
you into deeper *integrity*
than your relationship
with God.

Letting Go Before You're Ready

There's this upper room,
Right below the canopy,
Where I pray.

Sometimes face down
Other times, knees gripping the wood beams
That seem to be holding up my chest,
Between the moments lost
And the moments God makes good again.

The last time I cried was when I remembered how your thumb
Would hook to mine in the front seat,
I never told you but it always gave me goosebumps,
The kind that lingered with the buzzing oil of an innocent heat.

By the time this is published,
You'll be there and I'll be here.
And neither of us will know what's next.

I gave your love to the streams of Heaven,
Where the birds chirp for breakfast
And the owls coo in the morning dew.

Our ride felt like an unexpected dead-end,
We turned around multiple times until we realized
We just couldn't get through.

I heard the Holy Spirit say,
Just because it's great, doesn't mean it's Godly.

And I knew.
It was over before I could even get to you.

Letting you go has been the ultimate test of faith,
And my heart physically hurts each time I watch you walk away.

The worst part is when the elevator dings
And there's a painfully friendly hug at the 13th floor before you leave.

I'm learning the Lord doesn't always replace what He asks you to release.

Sometimes there's a tension as you sit through the in-between...

A waiting.
A yearning.
A trembling.
A trusting.

I call on Jesus in the aftermath of heartbreak,
But I wonder what would've happened if I said His name right out the gate.

When I first saw your brown eyes,
Poolside with nowhere to hide.
Sun bouncing off your eyelashes in the middle of the LA heat.
You were the last person I ever thought I would meet.

You said Christians were some of the greatest people you've ever met.
I held my cross in my left hand, wondering what would happen next.
Flash forward to your studio where we would walk away.
I buried the ache beneath my gaze, hiding what I wish I could say.

My eyes gripped you like a warning,
Knowing I'll choose God over the flesh,
every single day.

Even when it hurts.
Even when it doesn't make sense.

I'm learning this is the difference
between *having* faith and *being* obedient.

One asks you to open the door.
The other requires you to close it.

There's this upper room,
Right below the canopy,
Where I pray Christ reveals Himself to you
in a way that captures your whole heart.
More than I ever could.

And if it's in His Will,
maybe one day,
we'll meet again,
and that time,
our paths will align
and our moment
will be here to stay.

A Prayer for Encouragement

God,

Thank you for this body, this life, this moment.

Even though it feels rough right now, I bring You my weakness.
I trust Your strength and perseverance will be produced in me.

Thank you for filling me with love and patience as I enter the days ahead.

I surrender completely to You. Even though I don't know how to fully let this go, I will trust in Your Will and Your Way.

May You remind me of the path You've already set out for me.

May You remind me that You are walking *with* me, and that Your hand is on all of this.

Lord, You are my shepherd and in You, I lack nothing.

Remove any of the distractions in my mind so I can see through to Your faithfulness. I may not understand the reason You're asking me to let this go, but I can enjoy the process of coming to terms with everything that's happened.

I pray that You bring me back to the voice You've so graciously instilled within me.

I pray that clarity comes to me, surely and steadily.

In Jesus' name, I ask for support in softening my heart as I walk forward, letting go of any armor I've put up. I will not let shame keep me from You, Lord.

You are what matters most. You are above all.
You are miraculous, Holy, and Most High.

Fill me with Your presence, Your love, and shine into my soul, Lord, the only
way You know how. Holy Spirit – guide my steps, my words, and my actions.

Thank you for all the ways You support me, replenish me, and uplift me.
May I be an extension of Your grace and goodness.

Your love never fails, I know this for sure.
And even if I can't see it Lord, I trust that Your hand is on this.

Sharpen my discernment so I may see Truth.
My life is Yours and for that I am so blessed.

Thank you for making this day, this moment, this life.
Your joy is the source of my strength.

In Jesus' name I pray these words,

Amen

We don't pray for ease,
we pray for the *evolution*
our soul needs.

Unfolding Grace

Allowing something to unfold...
is the process of opening it *without* your hands.

Instead of hovering over it by force,
you spread out around it, and *experience* it by faith.

Without knowing how or why,
it blossoms from a wordless wonder.
To a distinct whisper.
To a gush of wind.

...Revealing a sequence of events that could only be woven together
by the Keeper and Creator of the universe itself.

I wonder what our lives would look like if we let them unfold,
instead of planning them.

If we unwrapped them like the sweetest gift,
instead of morphing them into boxes that could never fit.

Enjoying every edge, every taste,
and even savoring the places where two folds begin to stick.

I wonder what it would look like if we fully allowed God to *reveal* the next
steps to us, instead of insisting we know what the next step should be.

I've wondered why exactly we, as humans, hate being surprised. We detest
the unexpected and avoid the astonishing nature of being in shock and awe.
We're afraid of being *captured* by the awe. Typically we think of something
beautiful when we hear the word awe, but to be *captured* by something
means to be taken into possession without being in control.

Staying in control and having as much certainty and security is often what we yearn for the most. In that control, we think we'll be saved from any form of disappointment, heartbreak, shock, or grief. But control isn't your savior. Jesus is.

We feel most 'oriented' when we know what's behind us and in front of us. Yet, when we're in the present moment, the concept of a future and past gets reduced to *nothing*.

The here and now becomes all that there is.

I've found it's only in the present moment that God can shock us until we're completely *taken* in awe.

My prayer is that every human beckons the bravery necessary to experience that moment. I pray they memorize the feeling and pass it down for generations to come.

And if we can do that, God's story can be told through us forever.

"You show that you are a letter from Christ, the result of our ministry, written not with ink but with the Spirit of the living God, not on tablets of stone but on tablets of human hearts" (2 Corinthians 3:3).

Trying to measure and explain God leads you to miss out on experiencing God's profound presence—something *beyond* measure or explanation.

The Difference Between Testing and Temptation

There's a significant difference between a test and a temptation, but it's easy to confuse the two, because they both feel uncomfortable at times.

Tests are opportunities for growth, discipline, and refinement—they're tools God uses to build perseverance and character in us. Temptations, on the other hand, are the enemy's attempts to derail us, targeting our weaknesses and distorting our desires.

James 1:2-3 reminds us: "Consider it pure joy, my brothers and sisters, whenever you face trials of many kinds, because you know that the testing of your faith produces perseverance."

This shows us that perseverance isn't something we possess inherently—it's something God *produces* in us **through** testing. It's not instant or automatic, it's a cultivated characteristic.

Temptation exposes our doubt and our doubt exposes our double mindedness. To be double-minded is to be unstable (James 1:8). That word, unstable, stands out to me. It shows us that our feelings of instability aren't random or to be overlooked—they are rooted in a divided focus, a lack of belief in God.

The Relationship Between Testing and Temptation

God doesn't tempt us.

The enemy tempts us *during* a test. And often, the temptation only exists **because** the test is happening. If you stay near God through the test, it will further advance you and the enemy doesn't want that to happen.

One of my favorite quotes from Dr. Kuman says, *the biggest scheme of the enemy is tricking you that he doesn't exist.*

When I was deep in New Age Spirituality and occult practices, I saw how the enemy uses "love and light" spirituality to cloak truth in half-lies. New Age practices often perpetuate ignorance by encouraging us to blur the lines between good and evil under the guise of "oneness" or "universal love." These teachings can distort our discernment, suggesting that there's no need for boundaries, God's commands, or even acknowledgment of sin.

By minimizing the concept of evil, New Age Spirituality subtly aligns us with the enemy's greatest trick: convincing us that sin doesn't exist and that we are justified, perfect beings. This is particularly evident in practices like shadow work and manifestation. These practices often encourage us to see our sins not as something to repent from, but tools to achieve our desires. Shadow work might suggest that embracing our "darkness" or sinful tendencies is the key to self-empowerment, while manifestation can tempt us to use manipulation or sorcery to control outcomes.

The enemy's lie here is *subtle*: it reframes sin as a strength and distorts God's original design. We're led to believe that self-trust and self-love is the ultimate goal, rather than trusting in God and allowing His love to transform our hearts and desires to align with Him.

How Do You Know If You're Being Tested or Tempted?

God's tests will challenge you. The devil's temptations will ask you to sin.

Remember: temptation itself is not a sin. It's the tool used to get you to sin.

God's tests are designed to challenge us, to refine us, to produce something in us—whether it's discipline, love, perseverance, or trust. But temptation is the enemy's tool to derail us during the process.

God's testing calls us to rise; the devil's temptation tries to make us fall. The enemy will find personal ways to tempt you in areas where he knows you will thrive in God's plan.

As I reflect on my own temptations, they're typically around relationships and intimacy. If God is teaching me how to be a confident wife through the power of purity, patience, and contentment in His presence, I may be tested with a longer-than-comfortable-period of singleness.

The purpose of the test is to teach me how to stand in my God-given wholeness while breaking free of codependency and anxiously attached styles of relating. In this test, the enemy may tempt me with physical attraction (stepping out of celibacy) or relationships that aren't rooted in God's Will (men that aren't sent from God.)

This temptation isn't random—it's specifically crafted to appeal to my desire for connection, affection, and intimacy, even if it means living outside of God's design.

Of course, there's nothing wrong with wanting connection. However, when our desire requires us to sin, it's a deadly desire and not a Godly one.

But why does God test us? Because whatever lessons we learn through the test, we will need to steward the blessing He has in store for us.

That leaves us with a few questions:

- Why do we want to sin in the first place?
- Why do we want things outside of God's plan and design for us?
- Why do we feel lack?

The Anatomy of Temptation

If we didn't want something, the enemy couldn't tempt us with it. This truth brought me back to the garden with Eve in Genesis.

Imagine Eve in the Garden of Eden—a place of unparalleled beauty, overflowing with life and abundance. She walked freely among the trees, each one bearing fruit pleasing to the eye and good for nourishment. Every need she could imagine was met, and her communion with God was unhindered.

In this perfect setting, there was a tree, the tree of knowledge of good and evil. God said do not eat from this tree. This was God's boundary—a single command meant to protect, not withhold abundance. God established this boundary out of love and wisdom, knowing that humanity's flourishing depended on their trust in Him.

The tree of the knowledge of good and evil was not placed there to tease or deny Eve, but to offer her a *choice*—a chance to freely trust in God's provision and guidance. This boundary reminded Eve that while she lived in abundance, her dependence on God was essential for life and *true* wisdom.

By respecting this command, Eve would affirm her trust in God's goodness and sovereign wisdom. Eve was surrounded by evidence of God's abundance, yet this is where the serpent found her. The serpent planted the idea of lack in Eve's mind by asking a single question: "Did God really say, 'You must not eat from any tree in the garden'?" (Genesis 3:1).

Notice how the serpent used God's exact command but twisted it ever so slightly, so Eve would question what God *really* said. That question planted a seed of doubt for Eve, which birthed a sense of lack, and then her desire followed from that place. This reveals exactly how the enemy tempts us. First, he tempts us with a question that plants a seed of doubt. Then, that seed grows lack. Then, the lack creates a faulty desire that will have us stray from God. This is also how you can tell the difference between your desire and God's desire for you–if it requires you to stray from Him, then it didn't come from Him.

Here's where it gets crazy: once the serpent had a hold of Eve's perception, Eve started seeing the tree *through* the serpent's eyes—as something good, pleasurable, and full of gain. Instead of seeing the tree through God's command—a firm boundary that He said to not eat.

Seconds after the serpent had her perception, she sinned and ate from the tree. And for the first time, a bloodline of sin was born and brought into the world.

It's important to note that God did not create evil or sin. Instead, evil and sin arise when free will is misused, leading to choices that deviate from God's perfect will. God, in His love, gave humans free will to choose Him, but with that freedom came the potential for disobedience.

Remember, sin isn't "oh you did something bad, God hates you and is going to send you to hell." Sin is engaging in anything that separates us from God and His commands.

The enemy doesn't just tempt us with what's forbidden—he makes us believe we're missing out on something essential if we stay true to God's commands. He plants questions that distort God's truth and plan for our lives.

In my case, even though God's Word clearly says, "Do not be yoked together with unbelievers" (2 Corinthians 6:14). I've heard the enemy whisper, "Did God really say you can't date him though? Is dating really yoking?"

The tricky part here is that dating isn't inherently bad, nor is being friends with or engaging with unbelievers. But that's not the issue God addresses when He says, "Do not be yoked together with unbelievers" (2 Corinthians 6:14). To yoke means to couple or bind together. A yoke is a wooden crosspiece fastened over the necks of two animals, enabling them to pull a plow or cart together.

Now, imagine being yoked to another person. You're binding yourself to them and pulling something together. If one of you is chasing Jesus and carrying out God's assignment while the other is pursuing worldly desires and not acknowledging God's Will, you'll be moving in opposite directions. This mismatch creates tension and chaos, eventually breaking the yoke and the relationship.

God isn't saying you can't have relationships or connections with others. Instead, He's saying that when it comes to being yoked—forming deep, binding partnerships like marriage or other close relationships—it's crucial to be equally yoked. This means being aligned in your faith, moving toward the same shared vision within your personal relationship with God. By being equally yoked, you can walk in unity and fulfill God's purpose together.

The enemy knows all of this, so he's using God's Word, twisting it slightly and planting a question of doubt. And suddenly, I might find myself questioning

God's Word, focusing on a false sense of lack and a desire to live outside of His Will.

This sense of lack, leads to negotiating with sin and coming up with alternative ways to do it your way *and* God's way. This brings up the uncomfortable truth that not every desire you have is from God. Sometimes your desire is a byproduct of the enemy's distraction.

The Example of Jesus

Let's look at a different version of this. Because Eve and I and you aren't the only ones who are being tempted.

Jesus was, too. And yet, He's the only one who *never* sinned.

In contrast to Eve, Jesus shows us how to stand firm in the face of temptation. In Matthew 4, Jesus was tested in the wilderness after fasting for 40 days. I imagine after 40 days, He was very hungry. Any human would be. The wilderness was the *test*, but the devil *tempted* Him three times.

First, Jesus was tempted with the lack of food. "If you are the Son of God," he said, "tell these stones to become bread" (Matthew 4:3).

But Jesus didn't *respond* with sin.

He *rebuked* the temptation with God's Word.

He said: "It is written: 'Man shall not live on bread alone, but on every word that comes from the mouth of God.'" (Matthew 4:4) reminding us that the Word is both our defense and our weapon when faced with temptation.

Then, He was tempted with a lack of peace.

Then, He was tempted with a lack of power.

Here, Satan plants a question that attempts to poke at Jesus' position, posture, and who He is. The enemy operates the same way today as he did then. Planting questions that poke at our position, our identity, and our trust in God's promises.

How to Respond to Temptation

Remember, temptation can only offer *temporary fruit* that appears good, but leads to destruction.

When tempted, it is our responsibility to physically respond as Jesus did with the living Word. For example, when the enemy says: What harm could come from just dating?

I respond with:

- It is written…"I have the right to do anything, but not everything is beneficial" (1 Corinthians 10:23). *Yes, I have the right to date. But dating everyone is not beneficial.*
- It is written…"Whatever you do, do it all for the glory of God." (1 Corinthians 10:31). *Is what I'm about to do glorifying God? No.*
- It is written…"I am a temple for the living God." (2 Corinthians 6:14). *Is what I'm about to do honoring my body as a temple for the living God? No.*

Each response redirects my focus from the enemy's lies to God's truth.

Fixing Our Eyes on the Eternal

Temptation is temporary, but God's promise is eternal. "For our light and momentary troubles are achieving for us an eternal glory that far outweighs them all. So we fix our eyes not on what is seen, but on what is unseen, since what is seen is temporary, but what is unseen is eternal" (2 Corinthians 4:17-18).

If only Eve had fixed her eyes on God's promise—she would have recognized the serpent's schemes.

In your own journey, where are you learning to fix your eyes?

Even if you can't see God's full plan for your life, trust His Word. Trust that the test is producing something far *greater* than you can imagine.

Because oftentimes, an earthly *no* is a *holy yes.*

Temptation will always point to lack, but God's Word reminds us of His fullness. And when we trust in Him, we're not just overcoming temptation—we're stepping into the eternal glory He's prepared for us.

And *that* is worth the challenge.

Don't confuse God's
patience for slowness.
While you're waiting for
God to move you forward,
He's waiting for you to
walk back to Him.

The Unknown

Are you confusing the unknown for not knowing God?

Many people think that if they don't know the next step to take, then somehow they're failing. But we forget that God rarely reveals the whole plan to the passenger. Because in God's eyes, the unknown is not empty space—it's the most *fertile* space.

God often keeps things unknown because there are certain things that can only be understood and accessed through faith. Meaning, the more faith we have in God's plan, the more freedom we will experience in the unknown.

Imagine walking into a dense fog, unable to see even a few feet ahead. Logic and intellect may inform you of where you are, but faith gives you the courage to keep moving forward, trusting that the road continues even when it seems invisible. The unknown, then, becomes a gift rather than a grave. It's in the unknown that we can hear God the clearest, because in that space we become most dependent on Him.

When you walk by faith, you relinquish the role of the creator and step into your true role: the creation that God is moving through.

Jesus taught in parables during His ministry to reveal the secrets of the Kingdom. Why didn't He make it known right away? Why did He speak in riddles and stories instead of giving direct answers? Even His disciples asked, "Why are you speaking to them in parables?" Jesus replied, "Because the secrets of the Kingdom of Heaven have been given for you to know, but it has not been given to them" (Matthew 13:11).

This reflects the essence of the unknown: God reveals truths in *layers*, in His perfect timing. Jesus' parables acted as a filter, allowing those who sought Him earnestly to uncover the deeper meanings, while those who listened superficially missed the Kingdom's secrets.

In the same way, God's revelations often require us to lean into Him. As Isaiah 55:8-9 reminds us of God's declarations, "For my thoughts are not your thoughts, neither are your ways my ways." In the unknown, God invites us to seek Him—not just for answers, but for intimacy and understanding. It's in this space that faith is refined, and His glory is revealed.

There's a story of a woman in the Bible that always stays with me. She suffered from bleeding for twelve years, enduring pain, isolation, and countless failed attempts to find healing. I can't even imagine how she felt being in the unknown of what was happening, despite all of her efforts. She heard about Jesus' healing abilities in the unknown of her suffering and reached out in desperation, convinced that if she could just *touch the hem* of Jesus' garment, she would be healed.

At the time, Jesus was traveling by foot to heal the daughter of a synagogue leader. As He was moving through the crowd of people, the woman came up behind him and touched his cloak.

Immediately, her bleeding stopped.

She felt it in her body.

What's wild is Jesus felt it in His body, too.

This means, God can feel our faith just as much as we can feel His faith.

As she touched His cloak, Jesus realized that power had gone out from Him. He turned around in the crowd and asked, "who touched my clothes?"

Jesus kept looking towards the crowd of people to see who touched Him, the woman came and fell at His feet. He looked at her and said, "Daughter, your faith has healed you. Go in peace and be freed from your suffering" (Mark 5:34).

Jesus didn't address her as woman, person, or even you. He called her daughter. In doing so, He acknowledged her identity as a child of the Heavenly Father. This moment reminds us that, through Jesus, we too are given direct access to our Heavenly Father.

It was her faith that healed her, not walking towards Him. It is through our faith in Christ, that we are reborn as daughters of the Most High God, too. Think about that woman again. In her suffering, she met the power of Christ and was made whole. How stunning is that?

Even in the darkest unknowns, faith has the power to move us toward God's miraculous love and provision. She wasn't walking by herself, Jesus met her there. The unknown is not where God is absent, but where He waits for us to reach out, trusting in His power and love.

Will you step out in faith and believe that you are so deeply loved? Will you receive that love and allow God to guide you, even when the path is unknown? While Jesus came down as God in the flesh and is now resurrected back to the throne of God, He has given us His Holy Spirit. It is through the Holy Spirit that we are guided, comforted, and empowered every step of the way.

From this day forward, don't confuse the unknown with "God doesn't know me" or "I don't know God."

Let the unknown remind you that God's plan is always in motion, even when you cannot see it.

Let the unknown be the space where you surrender your answers and embrace His plan.

God never once guaranteed certainty, but our faith does.

Walk in faith and do not be afraid, for the unknown is <u>not</u> where God leaves you... it's where God comes to *meet* you.

"The Lord himself goes before you and will be with you; he will never leave you nor forsake you. Do not be afraid; do not be discouraged" (Deuteronomy 31:8).

Faith only moves the
mountain to the extent
that *you* are willing
to be moved by God.

there's a moment you realize God
has placed you in the *waiting room*.

and in your waiting,
you become like ember,
the softest part of the fire.

—*that reckless space between*

Doubt

Doubt is a peculiar force. When it creeps in, it can twist your mind, making you feel like you're standing on unstable ground. Doubt doesn't just linger—it grows, expands, and demands more attention over time. It has the power to consume us, unless we redirect it. And in those moments that doubt feels bigger than life, we're reminded to believe in an even bigger God.

Some days, it won't be your strength or determination that carries you through. Instead, it will be the realization that your doubt is pushing you to believe more boldly, to trust more deeply. Where the enemy tries to use doubt as a distraction, God will turn around and use doubt as an *indicator*. This indicator signals you're on the verge of stepping into something greater that will require a new level of faith—a level you've never accessed before.

When viewed through the lens of faith, doubt becomes a tool for *discernment*. It's not here to destroy your destiny but to shape it. It's a divine invitation to lean in and ask, "What's my next step?" When you confront doubt with faith, anything the enemy intended to use against you transforms into a testimony of God's power.

What if doubt isn't something to banish, but something to embrace?

What if doubt is a reflection of how big you're meant to play?

If your dreams were small, there'd be no room for doubt. If your life's mission was merely to stay within the confines of your comfort zone, you'd never feel the tension of uncertainty. Doubt arises because there is more for you to become. It's the evidence of a vision still alive within you, a dream yet to be realized.

Doubt can inspire action when we're not afraid of it. It's the nudge to get up and change what needs changing, to refine and align. It reaches into the depths of your being and reminds you: *there is still more work to do, you're not finished yet*. Instead of isolating yourself in the doubt, bring it to God so He can reveal His extraordinary capabilities.

When you become skilled at using doubt as contrast—to measure how far you've come and how far you're willing to go—you discover its true purpose. Resistance, after all, builds strength. Muscle memory is forged in moments of tension.

Doubt isn't a sign you lack faith; it's a sign you're being stretched to *walk* by faith. Without doubt, there would be no need for faith. The presence of doubt reminds us that we're walking paths beyond our understanding, venturing into territories that require His guidance.

And in those moments where you come face to face with doubt, don't fall. Look it squarely in the eye and declare: "Tricks on you. I'm walking into the room anyway."

You might shake and tremble as you speak, but you're not going to let doubt dismantle your destiny.

Doubt doesn't get the final say—your faith in God does. It's the fuel that drives you over mountains, across deserts, and through valleys. When you learn to use doubt as a companion rather than an adversary, you become unstoppable, a vehicle ready to drive on any road.

Doubt isn't the absence of faith—it's the very thing that *propels* it.

And in the end, it's not doubt that will define you; it's how you respond to it.

Will you let doubt paralyze you, or will you let doubt provoke you to believe bigger, dream wilder, and trust deeper?

The choice is yours.

"Do not be afraid" is *not* a suggestion; it's a command.

When we are obedient to this command, the unknown becomes fertile ground for God's story to unfold, a space where His glory can shine through our faith and trust.

The Miracle of Remembering

Sometimes life hurts. It comes with cracks and pains and moments that sting.

In the midst of the pain, there is always the miracle of *remembering*.

I hope you remember God's gaze is always upon you and in that, you are always taken care of, even if it doesn't seem like it in the moment. The days that feel like years will become mere moments sooner than you think, and the faster you surrender, the more you'll hear God speak.

I hope you remember that not every idea that comes to you is yours to execute, so listen for the call of God, not the command of your ambition. In your listening, you will learn to lead. The way you are called to lead, might not look like what you imagined. You might be surprised. Walk like God trusts you.

I hope you remember that when you are placed by God, there is no timeline. There is only where He would have you be, and your trust in His placement will reveal your next steps. Some days you will skip the line and other days you'll be on dusty knees, rough hands, tearing down seemingly immovable walls. Yet, through it all, God's grace will hold your belonging.

I hope you remember that wind doesn't always equal rain. And, yes it is safe to stumble and be swept up and moved beyond your comfort zone. It's the same trust you had to dream the dream in the first place that will hold you into the next chapter of your becoming.

With *that*, you are never starting over, you're always starting with God's grace.

I hope you remember that it is impossible for you to go back to zero, because that would mean you'd have to erase all the remarkable things God has already done *through* you and your life.

I hope you remember that fear turns into faith through prayer. And even on the days when you think you can't stand, it's better to have two knees on the ground kneeling in prayer, than nothing at all. When *all of you* is living for God's Will, forward becomes the only option and success is inevitable.

I hope you accept that you have changed and with that acceptance, courage swims and bravery speaks.

I hope you remember that in your humanness, God's Holiness can access you.

Where God goes, there you are. *Exhale.*

I hope you remember that sometimes joy comes in like a tidal wave swallowing sadness in one ancient breath, and other times it may feel more like the whisper of a flickering candle, barely burning. Drink up both, you'll never regret receiving the chance to smile.

I hope you remember how to rest, with your head buzzing and your bones breathing. God still loves you even when you're idle, staring into the ceiling until you hear what's next. This is what it means to be alive; blinking with hope at blank canvases.

I hope you remember that even though sometimes life hurts, that doesn't mean God hurts. The cracks and pains that sting our tender human heart, become throughlines for His Glory to bring you back to life.

Again and again. You are kept by an unfailing love that knows no end.

Never starting over, *always* starting with.

When One Door Closes

Sometimes one door closes
and another doesn't open.

Well then what?

What do you do when one door closes and it just... *closes*?

You're sitting in the void,
Like damp paper at the bottom of the ocean.
Like he's never calling you back,
Like there's no turning around,
Or escaping to another town.

You try to take a step forward,
But it doesn't set anything into motion.
Not like before, when you didn't have to fight for your devotion.

You used to turn red doors into blue skies,
You used to run ahead with your shoes untied,
You knew God would never leave you out to dry.

You were wet rain on the window,
You were fireflies in jars that glow,
You were the belly laughs when the wind broke.

Cheeks stretched, arms wide,
Like a dove flying at night.

Sometimes one door closes
and another doesn't open.
Sometimes the door just closes,
There is no second chance,

No next chapter,
Or happily ever after.

And then what?
Will you still believe in God's plan,
Or will you blame it on the time
It takes for you to understand?

I once thought taking God's hand
Was like walking on dry land.

Turns out it's swimming through a shoreless sea,
One that brings you to your knees,
One that digs up every wound
that hasn't healed and endlessly bleeds.

One that surprises you with popsicles in the Jeep,
No strap, just guitar strings that make you weep.

I once thought God's love was predictable;
Turns out that's a typo.
It's a wrist shaped concerto,
An amen as the wind blows.
It's my hand letting go of his cheek bone,
An ending that makes my prayers known.

Sometimes one door closes
and another doesn't open.

Instead, you wake up and learn to walk on ocean waves,
And you learn to breathe when the earth shakes,
And you turn your begging into benevolent faith,
And you stop asking how long it will take?

You plant your prayers in the trees,
And lick the tips of your furious needs,
All you can taste is honeyweed.

By now you've learned to savor the treat,
Of living in the great in-between, on the edge of defeat,
You let your heart become a reckless retreat,
Damp sheets and breakfast in the street.

And you wait, expectantly.
Like wet rain on the window,
Like fireflies in jars that glow,
Like a belly laugh as the wind breaks,
Cheeks stretched, arms wide,
Like a dove flying at night.

Sometimes one door closes
and another doesn't open
Eventually you wake up and see...

God isn't opening a new door, because He's building a whole new house.

"Yes, my soul, find rest in God, my hope comes from him. Truly he is my rock, and my salvation, he is my fortress., I will not be shaken" (Psalm 62:5-6).

God isn't opening a new
door, because He's building
a whole new house.

Patience Breeds Enthusiasm

God said... wait.

At least 119 times, His Word says...

Wait.
Wait.
Wait.

Stay where you are.

Until the proper time.

From Psalms, to Isaiah, to Acts, to Romans, to Galatians.

We're shown there will be moments in life where you *think* you're ready before God *knows* it's the proper time.

Waiting on God translates to moving for His Will. Waiting isn't passive. It isn't procrastination. Waiting in faith means preparing your heart, aligning your actions with obedience, and holding onto hope—even when the answers seem far away.

Think of Noah building the ark. He waited for the rain to come, but he worked in the waiting, trusting God's timing. Think of Mary's nine months before delivering Jesus. She waited, but her waiting carried purpose and expectancy.

Beyond waiting, God tells us to do it with *expectancy*.

There's hope in that expectancy: He will make it good in the end, regardless of how our circumstance or situation appears right now.

Waiting with expectancy means you trust God's promises so deeply that you live in *anticipation* of their fulfillment, instead of *anxiety* that it won't happen.

In our waiting, we believe that what God has promised is already on its way. Because where there is the Lord, there is order. A way better than our way.

And no matter how prepared you think you are, or how hard you're pursuing the achievement, person, or place... there's an internal shift that takes place. We embrace the quiet truth that it's not our pursuits that readies us, but our patience that readies us.

Patience stretches our faith. It reminds us we're not in control—and that's a good thing. When we wait, we acknowledge that His timing is better than ours. God isn't withholding out of cruelty; He's preparing us, shaping us, refining us. Scripture tells us that "He has made everything beautiful in its time" (Ecclesiastes 3:11).

While you're waiting, God is *making* everything beautiful in His time. The patience we cultivate in this time, transforms our spirit. It quiets the noise of our striving and sharpens our focus on God's voice. It's an absolutely essential foundation in a world that teaches us to rush, to hustle, to push until something breaks.

Patience breeds enthusiasm. The *real* kind.

Not for our plan or our timing...but, for God's timing.

Faith and Fortitude

God doesn't always use abundance to bless us. Sometimes the blessing is found in the training—the refining process that transforms adversity *into* abundance. It's in the hardest moments, when everything feels like it's breaking, that God is *building* something within us.

I picture myself sitting on a park bench after filing for bankruptcy, feeling lost and uncertain. I see myself on a plane to San Diego, tears streaming down my face after ending my engagement. I remember sleeping on my best friend's couch, unsure of where I'd live next. I feel the rolling waves of grief, the heartbreak of saying goodbye before I was ready. In those moments, blessings felt distant. All I could see was pain, loss, and obstacles that seemed impossible to overcome.

Yet, God's Word tells us otherwise: "We glory in our sufferings, because we know that suffering produces perseverance; perseverance, character; and character, hope" (Romans 5:3-5). And in James, we're reminded: "Consider it pure joy, my brothers and sisters, whenever you face trials of many kinds, because you know that the testing of your faith *produces* perseverance" (James 1:2-4).

Let's pause and reflect on the word *produce*. To produce means to bring something into existence that wasn't already formed. It's the act of creating something *new* from raw materials. In our trials, God is producing something in us that wasn't there before. He's using the raw material of our suffering to form traits we cannot cultivate on our own—traits like strength, wisdom, tenacity, patience, clarity, and discernment.

If we were already strong and equipped on our own, there would be no need for this process of production. God uses life's challenges to produce in us the very character traits necessary to steward the blessings He has planned for us.

There's a profound difference between being handed a piece of fruit and developing the skills to cultivate the character that steward and multiply the fruit. It's the contrast between receiving a blessing once and having the character to sustain it long term.

Take a moment to feel the difference, because the experience is an ocean apart.

God's blessings are not simply about the fruit itself, but having the fortitude to harvest in any circumstance. He doesn't just want to bless us; He wants to *prepare* us to carry, keep, and multiply His blessings.

In moments of suffering, it's not our power that turns adversity into abundance. It's God working *through* us. He is the one transforming trials into testimonies.

"And after you have suffered a little while, the God of all grace, who has called you to His eternal glory in Christ, will Himself restore, confirm, strengthen, and establish you" (1 Peter 5:10). This promise reminds us that God's goodness doesn't falter in our suffering. Instead, it transforms our suffering into fortitude.

Fortitude allows us to become a steward who can harvest in any season, under any condition. It's the strength to persevere, not just *with* abundance but *through* adversity. And in that perseverance, we become vessels of God's grace, equipped to carry His blessings far and wide.

Will you trust the process of refining, even when it feels like everything is breaking? Will you allow God to use your trials to produce something greater in you—something eternal and unshakable?

A Prayer for Purity and Peace

God,

Quench the ache inside my chest;
turn every desire into a *crashing wave* that unfurls into You.

Make my heart a shell of Your visions and dreams,
make my hands *ripple* with Your doing.

Lead me to the people You would have me serve,
guide my tongue to speak life on Your behalf,
wringing out all wickedness that lay dormant in my throat.

Wash away any shame, Lord.

Search me God for anything that isn't You,
And *dissolve it.*

Rapha, my healer,
Pour over me like water,
cleanse cleanse cleanse me Jesus.

Place the Will of the Father
at the center of my heart.

I pray and Heaven sings,
hear my song O God,
Know my heart.
For it is Yours.

In Jesus' Mighty and Majestic Name,

Amen

Faith says:

God, don't move
the mountain,
move me.

Your Grief isn't Holy

Your grief isn't holy; it's human. But how God takes pain and emptiness, and turns it into a reservoir of His unfailing love? That's Holy.

Grief is proof that God once loved through you so profoundly, it created an ocean inside your chest. It's a testament to how far and deep His love can stretch and expand the human heart, emptying it to make room for more of Him. Yet, too often, we romanticize grief. Clutching onto it tightly as a way to hold on to what was. Emotionally idolizing the past while forgetting the God who carries us through the present.

Consider the story of Jesus weeping. In John 11:35, we find the shortest verse in Scripture: "Jesus wept." It's a simple yet powerful reminder of His humanity and divinity colliding in one moment. Jesus wept not because He was powerless, but because He was present to the human emotion of grief. Jesus wept not as one overcome by grief, but as one deeply moved by the sorrow of those He loved. Jesus stood at the tomb of Lazarus knowing He would raise him from the dead, yet He allowed Himself to feel and express the pain of the moment.

And here's what we often overlook: Jesus' tears didn't define the story. His declaration did. Before we hear of Him weeping, He declares, "I am the resurrection and the life. The one who believes in me, even if he dies, will live" (John 11:25). His grief was real, but it didn't overshadow who He is. The grief wasn't the end—it was a passage leading to God's glory.

When we idolize grief or the person we are grieving, sometimes we forget who God is in it all. Grief becomes a monument to what we've lost instead of a testimony to who God remains. Grief tempts us to stay in the tomb, mourning what was, rather than stepping into the resurrection life God offers.

Emptiness doesn't have to mean pain or loss; it can mean you are *tender* enough to behold God's love. It means you are stretched by it, widened through it, and made a carrier of it. That emptiness *is* holy. Holiness isn't found in the grief itself but in how it transforms you, how it draws you closer to God and His love.

Grief is human, yes. But the way God meets you in your grief is divine. He doesn't leave you there. He weeps with you, while also calling you forward. As God says in Isaiah 43:18-19, "Forget the former things; do not dwell on the past. See, I am doing a new thing! Now it springs up; do you not perceive it? I am making a way in the wilderness and streams in the wasteland." He reminds you of who He is: the resurrection and the life, the God who turns mourning into joy, the One who makes beauty from ashes.

If you find yourself stuck in grief, ask yourself:

> *Am I remembering who God is?*
> *Or am I holding onto what was?*

When you no longer romanticize your pain, you can start trusting in God's power.

Grief stretches us, but it's not meant to define us. Let your sorrow remind you of the God who loves you so deeply that He enters into your pain and takes it as His own.

Let your loss widen you to carry His love more fully.

Let your grief propel you into the life He's calling you to live.

before God does work
through you, God does
work *in* you.

knowing the difference lives
in your *listening*.

A Capacity For Tension

Our capacity for tension is often far lower than our capacity for desiring the things we want. We crave the money, but resist the tension required to build the character to steward it. We long for the relationship, but avoid the tension of navigating the unknown as God prepares us for union. We yearn for success, but shrink from the tension of being 'on the way.'

Tension, by definition, is discomfort—a state where forces act in opposition. It stretches us, challenges us, and often feels unbearable. But tension is also the space where God refines us. Our relationship with Him will inherently carry tension—the tension between our ideas and His plans, between what we think we can handle and what He calls us to do.

Jesus taught us the ultimate lesson in tension.

Imagine if He had avoided the tension of the cross, the hatred, the misunderstandings, or the struggle of aligning God's Will with His human flesh. Redemption, forgiveness, the Holy Spirit, and eternal life would have been compromised. But Jesus embraced the tension, carrying it through to the moment He declared, "It is finished" (John 19:30).

That single moment of tension, birthed the greatest moment in the history of the world.

How often do we compromise with God instead of committing to Him? How often do we avoid the tension? And, in doing so, miss the threshold God designed to move His Will through us?

Tension isn't a punishment; it's a passage.

It's the means by which God stretches us to carry more of His spirit.

There is tension we create from stubbornness and drama, and there is tension designed by God to strengthen and stretch us. The difference lies in who you *seek* during the tension.

If you're processing a situation with five different people, it's likely a self-created drama triangle. But if the tension drives you to your knees in prayer, it's likely placed by God. No earthly counsel can resolve tension proposed by God; only the One who designed it can offer clarity and peace.

Tension reveals God's love when we seek Him first. It's not here to hurt us but to *prepare* us, to *build* trust, faith, and love. It doesn't always come with applause or rewards. It simply happens. The blessing isn't the resolution of tension; the blessing is the God Himself who we find through it.

When we surrender to tension, trusting His love, we stop resisting and instead, align ourselves with Him. In that alignment, suffering becomes temporary, a mere sensation rather than punishment. We find tenacity to move through life, syncing with God's design while setting aside our attachment to personal plans.

As Jesus endured the cross, tension gave birth to redemption and eternal life.

When we surrender to the tension, we increase our capacity to behold God's glory. And in that, the enemy's plans dissolve. All that is possible in God comes alive on earth, as it is in Heaven.

To die and be reborn in
the hands of God, brought
into life with Christ,
carrying His Spirit,
is the *greatest* gift.

Limitless Through God's Strength

Many of us fall for the trap of trying to live as an independent and limitless being. We're trying to be infinite, without bounds, attempting to dissolve our edges in search of that sensation of being absolutely nothing and everything at the same time.

We see this in practices and ceremonies designed to "raise our vibration," energy healing sessions that promise complete alignment, or even astral projection intended to transcend the physical realm. These pursuits often feed the illusion of limitlessness, whispering a promise of bypassing our flaws to tap into a boundless state of being.

And the funny part? It never lasts. Because it's a lie.

Our ambitious quest to become more, more, more limitless is actually our effort to become God. We think being limitless will allow us to achieve more success, avoid heartbreak, and somehow surpass any suffering.

Oh, how I have been humbled.

I'll never forget the day, while in prayer during my fast, my heart was pierced with a love I'd never experienced before. It completely saturated me and broke down every wall I had put up. It *did* feel like all of my edges dissolved, but this time was different.

This time, I was completely swallowed. Instead of feeling bigger, I felt small. Instead of feeling wider, I felt narrow. Instead of becoming boundless, I felt anchored. I didn't realize it at the time, but I was having my first encounter with Jesus. And, in all my limitations, I experienced the true limitlessness of Christ.

The truth is, it's never been about how far you can go or how big you can become. It's always been about how near you draw to Him and how big you allow God to become in your life. It's about how deeply you will love, depend on, and trust God as He moves in you.

It's not "I am limitless."

It's "I can do all things through Christ who strengthens me" (Philippians 4:13).

We all have limits no matter how much self-development work we do: physical, emotional, mental, and spiritual. These limitations are part of how God designed us as His creations. So, resisting our limitations leads us to also resist the One who created us.

Consider your physical limits for how long you can go without food.

Consider your emotional limits for how many people you can truly love, unconditionally. Consider your mental limits for how much you can read or write in one sitting. Consider your time limits for how quickly you can accomplish something.

One of our most obvious limitations is forgiveness. There are certain people, situations, and even parts of ourselves we cannot forgive without God's limitless ability to forgive *first*.

If we were truly limitless, we wouldn't need God, the only One who is infinite, holy, and boundless. Nowhere does God teach us that we are limitless.

Everywhere, He teaches us that we are limited and that we need Him.

Without God, we are incomplete. We cannot achieve anything truly fulfilling without His promise, His strength, and His covering. When studying the word limited, I learned that to be limited doesn't mean to be capped. To be limited means to be *without* fullness. The good news is, through Christ, we receive the Holy Spirit and are filled with the fullness of God.

At its root, the word "limited" points to a cross-path, a narrow road leading to the Creator. And so, limiting your flesh is not about deprivation but about discipline—an *intentional surrender* of earthly desires to align with God's Eternal Will. Through this surrender, we discover that self-discipline is not restrictive; it's *liberating*. It's when God stretches us and strengthens us to carry His Spirit more fully.

When you accept the discipline of limiting your flesh—whether it's resisting temptations, controlling impulses, or setting boundaries—you allow God to pour His boundless nature into you. This isn't about self-denial for the sake of suffering; it's about honoring God and making space for His presence. When you stop trying to outrun and surpass your limitations, you release into God's frame and take form in a completely new way. You'll begin reflecting His limitless glory into the world, becoming a display of His magnificence.

And in the end, you won't say, "I did it because I am limitless."

You'll say, "Thank you, God."

And that's the whole point.

"For nothing will be impossible with God" (Luke 1:37).

Conversations with God

Heavenly Father,

Who could ever replace You, when You alone are everything?
Who could rush Your brilliance?
Who could rush Your masterpiece?

I come to You and only You, for You are my maker.
My guide, my light, my anchor, my provider.

What do You want for me at this time?
What am I being prepared for?
What is best for the assignment You so graciously placed on my life?
What fulfills Your Will and ultimate plan?

I am Your daughter.
Wherever You go, I follow.
Whatever You want, I want too.
This is my confidence.

My fears dissolve in the depths of Your love.

In Jesus' Mighty and Matchless Name I pray,

Amen

When you realize God has forgiven you, it becomes *easier* to forgive yourself.

Finding God

Finding You took looking in the corners,
the cobwebs, the wood shelves,
the gray caves, the ocean floors.

All I can remember is wanting *more.*

I thought You were that meditation track,
the one that spun me round and round,
until I forgot which way was up or down.

I thought You were the tarot,
the one with temperance and arrows,
the charts filled with blue and gold,
seemed like truth, a mystery untold.

I thought You were quantum leaps
and manifesting a brand-new reality,
focusing on me me me,
and all my needs.

The devil tried to dress as You for fun,
but something inside of me said *run,*
so I left empty-handed, open palms, ready ears,
eyes thirsty for a You I didn't know was near.

I thought You were the jaguar
staring up at me from the dewey trees,
in the middle of *healing healing healing.*

The psychic handed me
another crystal to soothe my dreams.
Her answers comforted me

on the days I wasn't patient enough
to wait for the real thing.

Yet something inside of me
said get up and leave.
don't stop until you hear My name,
I promise you'll never be the same.

So I ran red lights and passed by trains
until cement turned to tiny grains,
Letting go of control and trusting what I could not see,
until there was none of me.

I thought my sadness made me cry,
but through Your joy, I began to weep.

My hands flew to the sky,
and I didn't have time to ask why.

Before I felt a shock of love,
like a lightning bolt,
that led to a velvet rope,
fruit and nectar
like milk and honey.

You sang through me like a music box,
reminding me where I left the lock.

And in that,
every missing piece of me,
Was restored back to the dream
My life now a display of Your masterpiece.

Turns out...

Read this piece out loud.

Right now, in this moment.

Even if it's a whisper with a trace of fog.

Let the vowels move throughout your body. Let the words find flight in your lungs. Let the sound of your own voice bring new sensations to life.

And then... repeat it, again and again and again, until you *believe* it.

Turns out there's a plan for me. Turns out there's not just a plan, but a whole destiny. And as long as that destiny is anchored in God, it's abundantly clear that everything is always working out.

Turns out I'm not starting over. Turns out I'm always starting *with*. I'm starting with everything God has fortified through me. I'm starting with God's strength and faith in me. I'm starting with the vision He's placed on my heart. I'm starting with the breath He's supplied my lungs. I'm starting with the voice He's given me. I'm starting with the gifts He's circulating through me.

Turns out nothing was taken. Turns out it's all being replaced with everything God sees for me. And in that, I am taken care of. And in that, I'm provided for. And in that, the Lord is my shepherd, I lack nothing (Psalm 23:1).

Turns out I am lovable. I let the Love of my Creator in. I let the love of being chosen by the Most High saturate and fill my thoughts. There is no part of me that could possibly be left behind. God will make His way through fire, rock, earth, and water for me. There are no walls He can't break down.

Turns out it's all happening. Turns out my past isn't holding me back. Turns out God is doing a new thing and He's asking me to perceive it. And so I will perceive and in my perception, I will believe. And in my belief, I will evolve. And in my evolution, I will become. And in my becoming, I will walk, fully and alive with the Spirit of the Living God.

Turns out there's a plan for me. Turns out I'm not starting over. Turns out nothing was taken. Turns out I am lovable. Turns out it's all happening better than I could ever ask or imagine.

Fully Free

It's the middle ground, just before you get to the good part.
It's crossing the street, left foot in front, with your hair down.

It's the yellow light about to turn green,
Before your foot touches the curb.
You wonder what it all means...

It's rebuilding, renovating, and receiving,
No longer wondering what everyone else is thinking.

It's the brink of faith backed by believing,
Arms stretched, lips wide, a *gentle* grieving.

It's on the road and in planes, scattered through the sky,
More questions than answers, you stopped asking why.

It's seeing the worst and still showing up with your best,
God sized vision, a valley of hope inside your chest.

It's seeing yourself before expecting the world to know your name.
Giving yourself permission to no longer stay the same.

Cold kiss, dark sands, what a life;
The *holy tension* you could cut with a knife.

It's dry paint on wood chrome,
Whispering into the shoreline, *there's no place like home.*

Body moving faster than doubt,
for once in your life,
you stop trying
to find a way out.

Leaning against a dimly lit tree,
you're remembering for the first time...
what it's like to be completely *free*.

The middle ground, just before you get to the good part,
Crossing the street, left foot in the front with your hair down.

It's the yellow light about to turn green,
The space between knowing and not needing
to know what any of it means.

—*whoever the Son sets free, is free indeed* (John 8:36).

Plateaus Are The Next Peak

When God isolates you, it's not punishment. It's preparation. It's creating an independent environment for your soul to evolve.

And yet, in those moments of isolation, we can confuse our experiences for being left behind, discarded, forgotten, or abandoned. We wonder what we did wrong or where we may have messed things up. But, God never leaves us. He is always there: present, quiet, and omnipotent.

God is beyond good; He is *great*.

And in His greatness, there is wisdom.

We can see this wisdom reflected in nature.

In mountains, we see life's challenges and with full faith in God, we can scale higher and move faster than we expected. In the desert, we see the vastness of unyielding space where God meets us in the unknown. In the lakes and oceans, we can appreciate the overflowing depth of His love.

And what about plateaus?

There's typically a negative association with this aspect of nature. In life, we tend to think that where there is a plateau, something is stuck. In nature, plateaus are flat, stable formations that offer animals a safe haven from predators. It's quite the opposite of stuck, if you think about it.

If we use this reflection in life, plateaus are a moment to pause, gather strength, and refocus without distractions. It's not that the activity in your life has slowed down or stopped—it's that the isolation is creating space for your vision to deepen and solidify.

Just as magma gathers and intensifies beneath a volcanic plateau, unseen momentum is building within you. Beneath the surface, heat and pressure are generating the energy needed for an eruption that will reshape *everything* around you. This phase is *essential* for something powerful to emerge. But for this to happen, you must stop making the *process* of the plateau wrong.

Have faith in who God has been *before the plateau*, and faith in who He is *beyond this moment*.

Sometimes, God places a plateau right in the middle of your journey for you to evolve. It's leverage, not a loss. It allows you to restore the resources you need for the next chapter.

You must recognize when God has called you into a season of stability. Stabilization is not stagnation. It's the foundation God is laying beneath your feet, preparing you for what comes next. And when that foundation is firm, it's time to scale again. It's time to climb to the next peak, to take the next leap of faith.

Remember, you serve a God who knows *exactly* what you need to take your life to the next level.

Trusting the process often means trusting the plateau. Don't let the enemy confuse your perception.

Even when you can't see it happening, God is moving mountains you didn't even know existed. Just because it's flat doesn't mean you're stuck. Often, it means you're about to take off.

Sometimes God will
isolate you to *evolve* you,
don't confuse being alone
with being left behind.

God Never Guarantees Certainty

God's never going to stop asking more of you.

The Lord said to Abram, "Go from your country, your people and your father's household to the land I will show you.

I will make you into a great nation,
And I will bless you;
I will make your name great,
And you will be a blessing.
I will bless those who bless you,
And whoever curses you I will curse;
And all peoples on earth
Will be blessed through you.

So Abram went, as the Lord had told him; and Lot went with him. Abram was seventy-five years old when he set out from Harran (Genesis 12:1-3).

In July 2017, I felt it: a pull so strong it would set into motion a chain of events I could never undo, only follow. I was 28, freshly unengaged, and living in Chicago—a city I had called home for six years, but now felt like a tightrope I was barely balancing.

One afternoon, I was sitting by the pool at my apartment complex, pouring my heart out to my best friend Tiffany, about the whirlwind of indecision, doubt, and hesitation swirling inside me. My plan was to temporarily move in with a girlfriend in Logan Square until I found something more permanent, though I wasn't convinced it was the right move. It felt like the *only* move.

And then, God's plan came out of nowhere. Tiffany said, "What if you came to San Diego? You could stay with me as long as you need. Maybe you'll end up moving out here."

I immediately got up and started pacing around the pool. San Diego? The thought hadn't even crossed my mind. Yet, within moments, I had American Airlines pulled up on my phone. It was as if my body had said a *holy yes* before my mind could catch up.

A few weeks later, I packed my belongings into two bags and boarded a one-way flight to San Diego. I didn't know what to expect or if it would work out, but for the first time in a long time, it felt like I had nothing to lose.

In hindsight, I can see how God was present in that decision, though I wouldn't come to build a relationship with Him until five years later. It's amazing how God pursues us, before we ever pursue Him. I'm in awe of how He is truly always with us, preparing a way for us to open our eyes and see the Truth.

This reflection brings to mind Abraham's journey in Genesis. Abraham was 75 years old when God called him to move. Yet, I often wonder how many smaller calls Abraham received that prepared him to move by absolute faith for that one move that would shift the trajectory of everything. How many times did he say holy yes in the quiet moments when no one else was watching? How often did he continue to pray, even when it felt like no one was listening?

Abraham's story reveals a heart postured in trust and obedience—a belief in God's promise over his own plans. God didn't give him a detailed roadmap. Instead, He gave Abraham a *promise*: "I will make you into a great nation" (Genesis 12:2). Abraham didn't ask for all the answers; he simply listened and moved. He left everything familiar to journey into the unknown, trusting that God's plan was greater than his own understanding.

This is the nature of faith. God doesn't promise certainty, yet our faith in Him *does*. You may wonder, "How do I know if it's God's plan or my own?" The answer is simple: when you don't care if anyone else sees it but Him, *that's* God's plan. When you don't need answers to move, because you trust His promise, that's God's plan. When you're not rushing but waiting on His timing—the timing of the God who created the universe in six days—that's God's plan.

If Abraham had split his focus between listening to God and listening to "source energy" or false gods, he would have been confused when the call came. God didn't design us to depend on other sources or to move by our own strength. He designed us to hear His Word, and in our listening, we pack, we step, and we go.

Through Abraham's story, we see that God doesn't ask if we're ready or check to see if we're comfortable before He calls us. When God is ready, that means we are too. Instead of asking God *for details*, Abraham answered with a footstep. Instead of asking how, Abraham trusted God's promise. God doesn't give us the how—He turns us into the how. As we are shaped by Him, we become the blazing evidence of God's glory.

But, before God does work through us, He does work in us. For 75 years, God was working in Abraham before He worked through him. This reveals the nature of God: everything is done with intention and preparation.

So when we start to question the speed of God's plan, we must remember this truth: God doesn't see time as we do. Scripture reminds us, *"With the Lord a day is like a thousand years, and a thousand years are like a day"* (2 Peter 3:8). The God who created the universe in six days—establishing galaxies, oceans, and life itself—knows more about timing, pace, and preparation than we ever could. His delays are not denials; they are *intentional preparations* for what He has already planned.

When you remember that your life was created for His glory, everything He wants for you becomes what you want, too. This is the gift of faith: a steadfast certainty that no matter how long it takes, God's timing is perfect, and He makes all things good.

Who knew that one-way ticket would lead me, five years later, to sitting in Church saying yes to a fast that would forever transform my heart. I didn't know, but God did.

Faith is not about demanding clarity in the plan, but trusting completely in the One who holds it. He says, "Move," and you answer with a footstep, even when you don't see the full picture. Because faith isn't about waiting for certainty—it's about moving *with* certainty in the One who created you.

A Prayer for Strength and Surrender

Come unto me Lord, my heart opens with praise for Your mercy and goodness.

How holy You are, how just You are, how righteous You are.
A perfect stream of holiness, my faith swims towards You and You alone.

No other could compare to Your matchless Glory.
The battle is won through You, that I trust.

Thank you Holy Spirit. When I cry out, You come.
Your love never fails. Your love, the only love, that can swallow fear.

Your love, the only love that saves. That fills me to complete wholeness.

My praise I give to You Lord, my heart I lay at Your feet.
My faith strengthens in Your hand.

Sculpt and shape me into an image bearer,
holding the wordless wonder of Your Will.

May my life be a reflection of Your goodness,
as You make my spirit stronger.

When I feel weak or afraid, help me lean into Your frame.
I walk in big faith. Bounded by Your Word.
Guided by Your Way. Filled with Your love.

Thank you, Jesus.

In Your Mighty and Matchless Name I Pray,

Amen

Prayer *covers* what God
has in store for you with
unwavering faith.

This is How I Fly

even when it hurts,
i'll call out Your name.

i look and there You are
windows foggy with wonder
a burning bush
whispering smoke
that wraps me in a memory
of all the times You made
the rain feel like fireworks.

even when it hurts,
i'll seek comfort in
Your Word.

the deeper i swim
the less i know how
and there You are
scripture dancing like
wind-chimes in my head
tangled in a velvet light
that breathes across
the ocean floor
untamed
yet anchored.

this is how i fly.

with a slightly broken wing
ten toes down
a heart drenched in hope.
i remember You never left.

i remember that i belong in You.
even when it hurts,
i'll praise Your goodness.

swimming upstream
the sun bends at my feet
pointing arrows at an open sky
like fireflies finding their way
through the night.

even when it hurts,
i'll rest in the peace of Your
immaculate nature
glazed in truth,
from sand to rock
i sense Your knowing.

a turning tide,
each time i'm on the brink of asking why
my throat lingers with a sweetness
that reminds me innocence isn't earned,
because it was never lost.

and there are no questions,
when You, my God are the answer.

so even when it hurts,
i'll take Your hand.
i'll call out Your name.
i'll seek comfort in Your word.

and i'll rest in Your perfect peace.

When the Creation Runs Back to the Creator

When we put effort into knowing God and stewarding His Kingdom, it goes beyond achieving earthly rewards or recognition. Our relationship with Him is rooted in eternal significance—a purpose that transcends anything this world can offer.

The work we do, the choices we make, and the lives we impact are all part of a greater story, one that echoes into *eternity*. God doesn't call us to excellence for fleeting applause but to align us with His eternal design and to glorify Him in all we do.

With that, God's Word will hold you to a higher standard than your own standards ever could or that the world ever would.

Yet so many people are in an auto-pilot relationship with God. It's a relationship that exists in their life but isn't *alive* in their heart. Because when God is alive in your heart, there's a change in behavior. There's a change in desire. There's a change in how much effort you put into honoring Him.

I'll never forget when my dear friend Izabella Gorré said to me in conversation, "there's a big difference between believing in God and honoring God." I believe our generation is currently facing this difference and my prayer is that we decide to not just believe in Him but honor Him with our bodies, our actions, and our behaviors. To honor God requires surrender—a willingness to let Him guide every part of our lives.

And yet, there are still the ones who make every decision on their own. They pick and choose when God gets let in and when He doesn't. They decide what their life looks like, what direction they'll take, who they'll date, what they'll tolerate, who they'll have sex with and how soon they'll become intimate. They decide what they feel is best for their career, how to love, how to forgive, how to fight, how to stay, and how to walk away.

Now, imagine giving birth to a body of creation. One day, that creation acts as if the One who created them wouldn't have any knowledge about how they're designed to live and what would be most fulfilling for their heart.

Instead, the creation's entire life is decided by their flesh and God (the Creator) exists in the background as a subtle note that's *barely* heard.

It pains God to watch that creation, and how their life unfolds.

The creation experiences a limited scope of who God is and just how miraculous He is, above anything else. Or worse, they try to become God themselves.

And then when they get fired from a job, or their loved one passes, or the friendship ends, or the person they thought was their soulmate leaves, and life twists in an unexpected way...

They discover that the drinking stops working, and finding validation in other people stops working, and the money stops working, and the success stops working...

The creation gets jolted by the striking reality: they actually *do* need their Creator.

So they run to Him.

And they cry out, confused and claiming they can't hear him. They wonder why they can't tell the difference between God's voice and their own — after *years* of only listening to their sin as the standard for their life.

Yet even with that, God's unfailing love reaches the hardest hearts, guiding them to Jesus–God in human form. Jesus came to live among us as the Son of God, sent to save us and redeem us from our sin and lust for the world.

Jesus lived on earth to show us how to have a personal relationship with God, creating a path for all people, in every generation and nation, to have direct access to our Heavenly Father.

Before returning to the throne of God, Jesus declared that He is the way, the truth, and the life—the only path we were created to follow—and He promised His peace to those who believe in Him, a peace not as the world gives, but one that calms troubled hearts and conquers fear (John 14:27).

And when the creation accepts Jesus as Lord and Savior, they receive His Spirit—the Holy Spirit—who lifts us up, sets us apart, and empowers us to live in freedom, walk in truth, and fulfill God's purpose for our lives.

The beauty of the gospel is that it's never too late to turn back to your Creator. God's arms are always open, His love unshaken, and His grace sufficient. But the question remains: will you wait until everything crumbles to run to Him, or will you invite Him into your life now, fully and completely?

Imagine what your life could look like if you stopped trying to live by your own strength and let the One who designed you lead the way. Imagine the freedom of surrender, the joy of being anchored in God's purpose, and the peace of knowing you are held by a love that never fails.

God isn't in the background, waiting for an invitation; He's been pursuing you all along. The only thing He asks for is your *Holy Yes*.

So, will you trust Him? Will you let go of control, let Him shape your heart, and guide your life? The choice is yours, but the promise is eternal: through Jesus, you are redeemed, restored, and made whole.

There is only one option: God's Will.

And when you make His Will the only option, you make success *inevitable* because God already won.

A Prayer For Your Relationship With God

Heavenly Father,

Thank you for this day, this life, this moment with You.
May every moment of today be in reverence of my relationship with You.
May today be a reminder that nothing is lost when it comes to You.
Everything can and will be used in Your glory.
Thank you for the discernment to know Your plan above my own.

I am here to follow Your footsteps and walk steady with Your Word as my guide.
Fill me with Your peace Lord, the only peace that could ever quench my thirst.
And as each moment unfolds God, You are the One who sustains me.
You bring me vitality to move forward with laser sharp focus, and unwavering purpose.
And as You move, I listen. I rest on the island of peace that You've given me.
Meet me in the moments in between.
I will seek You through the noise and I believe Your voice will find me.
You are with me always Lord, and in You, I have everything.
Not my will but Yours to be done, on Earth as it is in Heaven.

In Jesus' name I pray,

Amen

Live as if you're just a *footstep* outside of Heaven.

...and watch who you become in the presence of the Most High.

A Prayerful Life

i don't want to just live a life.
i want to live a *prayerful* life,
one dripping in holy tension.

with the edge of need,
complete dependency,
on the King of peace.

when i speak
i don't want to just make a sound,
i want to feel like i'm using God's paintbrush,
like i can't put the pen down,
like it's an honor to begin *again*.

and when the page turns,
my footsteps will burn
the past into bits of glory.

no, prayer is not begging,
it's a vow.
a testament to your faith,
right now.

prayer is reminding you
of all the ways God moves
in you
only to get *through* you.

prayer is gathering all of your uncertainty,
and turning it into *poetry*.

it pulls you forward like a riptide,

where you can no longer hide,
in the sandstones of silence.

and if you pay close enough attention,
you'll see prayer is not only about receiving,
it's listening *and* believing.

prayer reveals God's plan
to the ones who are *brave* enough
to dream on their knees.

–from begging to becoming.

Faith Isn't a Feeling

When you give your heart and your life to Christ, you no longer belong to the world, and you no longer belong to your flesh—your feelings.

Read that again, because this is *incredible* news.

Each of us has been trained in some way to have more confidence in our flesh than faith in God. That's why, in Christ, we're called to "set [our] minds on things above, not on earthly things" (Colossians 3:2). We're instructed to "put to death whatever belongs to [our] earthly nature: sexual immorality, impurity, lust, evil desires, greed, which is idolatry" (Colossians 3:5). Instead, we come under God's nature, His Will, and His character—not to serve our own self-interest but to advance His Kingdom.

One of the most challenging revelations I've had to accept is this: just because you feel it, doesn't mean it's holy.

In a self-help-fueled world that glorifies feelings as facts, this can be a daunting wake-up call. What happens when your feelings lead to lust? Or when your feelings are subdued by sexual immorality? What about when you feel unworthy?

God shows us the difference between feelings and beliefs throughout His word.

Picture this:

> Your thoughts are like seeds, growing roots that eventually turn into beliefs.

> A thought can only become a belief if you water it long enough.

> Within that, your feelings are like temporary weather patterns,

changing daily. *Let them.*

Feelings stem from the flesh. Beliefs stem from a sound mind.

Feelings were never meant to lead. They're meant to be experienced.

The real challenge emerges when we allow our feelings to dictate our beliefs. This can look like: *feeling* attracted to a certain practice or artist or food that isn't bringing you closer to God. And soon, you believe in it more than you believe in God. You *feel* sad or rejected, and soon you believe you're alone. This is precisely how the enemy sneaks in, using our feelings to plant roots of unbelief that pull us further from God.

But "God has not given us the spirit of fear; but of power, and of love, and of a sound mind" (2 Timothy 1:7). Will you believe that, even when your feelings tell you otherwise?

To illustrate this, consider Jesus in the garden of Gethsemane. On the night before His crucifixion, He experienced deep anguish and sorrow. These are real feelings. "My soul is overwhelmed with sorrow to the point of death," He said (Matthew 26:38). In that moment, Jesus felt the *full weight* of human emotion—fear, sadness, pain. Yet, He did not let those feelings dictate His belief or His obedience. Instead, He prayed, "My Father, if it is possible, may this cup be taken from me. Yet not as I will, but as you will" (Matthew 26:39).

Even in His deepest sorrow, Jesus' faith overrode His feelings. He trusted God's plan and surrendered fully to His Will. This is the perfect example of walking in faith, not feelings. When we stand rooted in our belief in God's Word, His unfailing love, and His perfect will, we grow in intimacy and trust with the One who created us, knows us, and chooses us. In that intimacy, it becomes safe to feel—but those feelings no longer interrupt our identity. Our feelings no longer breed suffering that pulls us from Him, instead they deepen our dependency on Him.

Walking in Christ means walking by faith. You allow the peace of Christ to rule in your heart (Colossians 3:15). As you mature in your faith, you learn to experience feelings without letting them change what you believe. Over time, God produces in you a confidence that can withstand any storm—a peace that surpasses understanding (Philippians 4:7).

As one of my favorite worship songs says:

> "Faith is more than feeling. It's like seeing the invisible. Somehow I see it, all that lies at the end of the road. And I don't know the timing, so I'm guessing it's not mine to know. Lord, help me *believe* it. All those days when I feel like I don't. I've learned faith isn't fearless. It's just trusting when you fear the most."
>
> – Benjamin William Hastings, *Homeward*

Notice the words say: "Lord, help me *believe* it," not "help me *feel* it."

Your feelings are temporary reactions of your flesh. Your beliefs are the roots that bind you to God's nature. And when the going gets tough, it's not what you feel that will move the mountain—it's *who* you believe in.

I pray that God shifts your belief in this moment, and that the whole atmosphere changes with it. Because faith isn't built on feelings; it's built on the firm foundation and belief in God's Word.

There's never any risk in *having* faith;
what's risky is **acting** by that faith.

You lose nothing by having faith,
and risk everything by acting on it.

But wherever you're going,
as long as it's closer to God,
it's worth it every time.

– *make your move.*

Your courage makes
your faith complete.

Don't just think about it,
believe about it.

The sensation of desire wakes me up at night.
I'm holding on but longing for
the waves to lift the tide
and meet my toes

where the dripping cold
will rock the shock of hope
inside my chest.

It's been two years
and some months since
I closed the door to lust.

Yet, I'm longing in that wild way where,
even the hair on my skin
tastes like cinnamon.

I sip the air between my lips
and I pray with God as the moon slips
a goodbye to the star of the sun
and I'm choosing being chosen over chasin'

So I'll stay,
close to Yahweh
with my head in the lap of a King.

Breathing with a hallelujah
under a bed of peonies;
I won't look back as
I open the gates of purity.

—celibacy

If you think your sadness
makes you cry, watch when
your joy makes you *weep*.

The most vulnerable
emotion to show isn't pain,
it's the wild joy of the
Holy Spirit.

Healing Through The Holy Spirit

Growing up, I held so much anger and resentment towards my father. Our home environment was oftentimes tense and unpredictable. I learned to move cautiously and tiptoe through uncertainty, choosing to silence my voice and emotions—and over time, it became a profoundly heavy weight that often left me teetering.

We went through many ups and downs throughout my childhood. By the time I was 19, I refused to speak to him. For almost a year, he called daily and I couldn't bring myself to answer. Where I used to feel weak, I felt powerful in my silence, using my lack of communication as punishment. Silence became both a shield and a weapon.

Towards my mid-twenties, I felt safe enough to let him back into my life. After all, he was in Michigan and I was in Chicago. Physical distance meant he couldn't really be part of my life, and multiple yards of emotional distance meant I never really had to let him in, and he never really knew who I was. Our conversations remained surface-level, and yet, I was always on edge waiting for him to say something that would fire-off a code red in my body.

As we began speaking more, I noticed I would have this recurring dream where I was rage-screaming in his face. I mean, full on, Stage 5 Raging Explosion. In the dream, I couldn't make out anything I was actually saying, but I was defending myself for all the years where I felt like I didn't have a voice. I was screaming all the insults I wished I had the courage to say in the moment when the original pain was happening. And I was pounding on his chest, trying to get him to feel just a *sliver* of the hurt and resentment I'd been carrying all those years. When I would wake up, my heart would physically hurt and my fingers tingled with aggression. I was *furious*.

Yet, when we talked on the phone, I hid the anger as if everything was fine. I pushed the anger down as far as it would go, until it became a foothold for the devil. Soon that anger would turn into resentment, and then that resentment turned into pride. Yet, underneath that pride was a deep well of sadness, pain, and grief.

I went to every New Age healer I could find to attempt to "energetically move" the anger and the pain. Some tried to alchemize the anger with sound or rattles, or perform "psychic surgery." Others would put crystals on my "chakras." Others would have me talk to my inner child or channel guides and spirits to help reconcile the pain. At one point I even opened my "Akashic Records" where I was told my dad and I had an agreement in a "past life" that we were meant to wrestle through in this life. It all felt *neverending*.

Each of these only offered temporary reprieve. They attempted to give me "answers" for why I was angry or why our relationship felt so difficult, yet none would completely dissolve the feeling of wanting to rip my insides out—because none were the real Truth.

Later on, I would discover that the little 8-year-old inner child and spirit guides I was seeing during all the "healing" were really familiar spirits. Familiar spirits are demonic entities that mimic people, emotions, or circumstances to deceive and manipulate us into cycles of bondage. They often appear as something comforting or known, drawing on memories or fears to gain access to our lives.

Each time I emerged myself in these healing modalities, I was unknowingly bonding with demonic agendas. They kept me stuck in a perpetual "healing" loop, always searching for freedom but never finding it, because I was leaning on a counterfeit instead of the true Healer.

Years later, after I gave my life to Jesus, I finally began to understand the difference between counterfeit healing and the real thing. I learned about and received the Holy Spirit, the true source of freedom and healing.

The Holy Spirit is the third person of the Trinity, fully equal and eternal with the Father (God) and the Son (Christ Jesus.) While God is the Creator and sovereign planner of all things, and Jesus is the Redeemer who took on human form to save humanity, the Holy Spirit is the presence of God actively working in the world and in the lives of believers.

Unlike the counterfeit healing methods I had pursued, Jesus, through the Holy Spirit, doesn't offer quick fixes or surface-level solutions. Instead, He works deeply, uncovering the roots of our pain and leading us to the Truth that *sets us free once and for all*. As John 16:13 writes, "When he, the Spirit of truth, comes, he will guide you into all the truth." And as 2 Corinthians 3:17 reminds us, "Where the Spirit of the Lord is, there is freedom."

After Jesus was crucified, resurrected, and ascended to heaven, He sent the Holy Spirit to be our helper and guide. In John 14:16-17, Jesus promises, "I will ask the Father, and He will give you another advocate to help you and be with you forever—the Spirit of truth. The world cannot accept him, because it neither sees him nor knows him. But you know him, for he lives with you and will be *in* you."

This is the gift you receive when you give your life to Jesus—the presence of the Holy Spirit dwelling *within* you. It wasn't long after surrendering my life to Christ that my entire body, mind, and heart began to change before my eyes.

When we choose to live by the Spirit rather than the flesh or counterfeit spirituality, we experience an entirely new way of being—one that reflects God's nature. As Galatians 5:22-23 explains, "But the fruit of the Spirit is love, joy, peace, patience, kindness, goodness, faithfulness, gentleness, and self-control." These are not traits we can produce on our own, but are the evidence of the Spirit working within us.

Now, you may be wondering, *"How do I know it's the Holy Spirit and not a familiar spirit or something else?"*

Or maybe you've reached temporary states of joy and peace on your own. Always look at the *fruit* that's been produced. Someone could say they've forgiven or let go or have grown from something, and yet the fruit they're producing is chaos, gossip, and drama. Before, my "healing" led me down a spiral of never ending loops. I was always searching, trying the next modality, manifestation script, or affirmation but never finding *true* relief. I would go on these spiritual highs where everything felt great for a moment, only to crash again into the same cycle. Because until my *heart* changed, nothing else would actually follow that change.

In contrast, the Holy Spirit brought true healing and peace. Giving my heart and accepting Jesus as my Lord and Savior expanded my capacity to forgive and deepened my ability to love—because I was no longer trying to heal myself through modalities, relationships, and substances. Now, it was His Spirit working *within* me.

The resentment and bitterness I once harbored began to fall away. The tormenting thoughts of anger and rage were replaced with clarity and rest. I held within me a deep patience and compassion I had never known or thought was possible. Ultimately, a new desire was born inside my heart: a desire to reflect Christ in everything I say and do. A desire to love in a completely new way.

The more I leaned into the truth of the Gospel, the more simplicity I felt. Healing was no longer complicated or earned, it was a natural byproduct of giving my whole heart to the Lord. This is the work of the Holy Spirit: aligning us with God's Will, refining our hearts once and for all, and enabling us to live as vessels of His grace and love.

One afternoon, I felt the Holy Spirit prompt me to begin praying for my father. I don't even know where the words came from, but I began speaking life over my father and our bloodline. Instead of praying for the anger to go away or for my father to change, I brought God my anger instead. I began praying for the Holy Spirit to fill me to the brim with a love so deep, that it would swallow all fear. I prayed to be moved in a way that was unrecognizable to me.

The Bible says, *in your anger do not sin. Do not let the sun go down while you are still angry, and do not give the devil a foothold* (Ephesians 4:26-27).

When I read this scripture, I hear God say: your anger will tempt you to sin. Feel it, but do not identify with it. When you identify with the anger, you feel more justified to sin in it. In my case, sin looked like pride - *an uncontrollable desire to be right*, cursing - *using language that spread darkness*, wrath - *holding on to intense anger*, and idolatry - *worshiping something other than*

God.

This verse also shows us that anger gives the devil a foothold. A foothold is a place where a person's foot can be lodged to support them in climbing up, so our anger gives the devil support to climb up into our lives and plant seeds of darkness.

The darkness and anger built up so much resentment, I ended up using alcohol as a way to self-medicate and suppress how I was really feeling, and turning to false gods to find relief.

What if instead of sinning in our anger, we *submitted* our pain, frustration, and anger to Jesus instead?

In moments of anger and frustration, we can find ourselves overwhelmed by deep, heart-wrenching desperation. I've been there, and I know many can relate to this raw and vulnerable place. Yet, there's something truly miraculous about this kind of desperation—it can quickly turn into some of the most *powerful devotion* when turned towards the hand of God. Because ultimately, it's all for His glory.

When you come through the pain, it's God's name you'll glorify on the other side–not your own, not a healer or guide that came to you. Desperation doesn't have to consume you, nor is it something you have to fix or carry by yourself. It's an invitation to surrender and let God move in your life.

Over time, it was as if God had given me a new heart. I began to see my dad differently, to hear him differently, and to forgive him in a way that was no longer tied to the weight of my own pain.

Jesus, through His time on Earth, modeled us the perfect way to forgive. He showed us that forgiveness isn't about accepting or justifying what happened—it's about releasing the grip of what *didn't* happen, the unmet expectations, and the unhealed wounds. It's about stepping into a perspective that transcends our fragmented, human view.

Through the Holy Spirit, we're empowered to see the person or situation through God's eyes—a lens of grace, compassion, and love that goes beyond the natural and into the *supernatural.*

True forgiveness of someone else always makes its way back to our own hearts. It becomes less of an act to be the bigger person and more of a gift to become a new person—a reflection of Christ in us. As I began to forgive my dad, I saw this mirrored in my own heart. The more I forgave him, the more I forgave myself.

And I can't remember the last time I had that recurring explosive dream.

Today, I consider my father one of my very best friends. I can trust him with my biggest business ideas and turn to him for support and guidance. I can laugh with him until we're both in tears, and I can be honest with him about what's on my heart, without holding it in.

Just a few months ago, we were sitting together in the middle of Times Square to view a Billboard I'd been featured on. I looked at him across the sea of lights and said, "Who would have thought we'd be here? We've come such a long way." He looked at me with gratitude.

Later that evening, I shared with him that as much as my heart had changed, I saw the Holy Spirit move in him too.

Without words, we had an entire conversation that can be summed up with one powerful name...

Jesus.

Not even anger can tear His love apart.

"Peace I leave with you. My peace I give to you. I do not give to you as the world gives. Don't let your heart be troubled or fearful" (John 14:27).

there's a version of you
who never dreamed you
would dream *this dream*,
but God did.

Loving God in Overflow

One of my favorite worship songs, Easy by Elevation Worship, writes, "*I'll keep finding a billion ways to show you, just how much I love you.*"

The beautiful thing about God is that loving Him comes with more love. Yet we tend to focus our attention on loving others in an effort to receive the same love they're giving. This is always a gamble. There are no guarantees or certainty in how other people will show up or respond.

Loving others in that way isn't really love; it's a *conditional* exchange. It's a counterfeit language that speaks more to one's own needs than genuine and unconditional love.

Now imagine this:

You redirect all that effort, energy, and longing towards loving God, who loves you *unconditionally*. You pour your energy and devotion into loving Him in all of His goodness and glory, needing nothing in return—no chasing for validation or acceptance. It's pure love.

You recognize that you are already loved, beyond measure, simply because He created you. His love is unfailing and unchanging. The more you pour into your relationship with Him, the more you become filled with His love.

This naturally transforms how you love others.

Loving people is no longer about trying to get them to love you back. Instead, it's about sharing the *overflow* of God's love that's already within your heart. You love without conditions, without expectations, and without needing anything in return.

You love because you are simply resting in His love.

God is love.

As the apostle John writes: "Dear friends, let us love one another, for love comes from God. Everyone who loves has been born of God and knows God. Whoever does not love does not know God, because God is love" (1 John 4:7-8).

And later, John reminds us that, "No one has ever seen God; but if we love one another, God lives in us and his love is made complete in us" (1 John 4:12).

When we love each other, we make God visible. Our love becomes the evidence of the Holy Spirit, flowing through us and out into the world.

When you root yourself in this holy love, your perspective on relationships transforms. You no longer seek fulfillment from others because God's love is all-sufficient. You no longer feel the emptiness of unmet expectations because His love fills every gap.

You love freely, generously, and joyfully. There's no strings attached, because you know that God's love is endless.

You're grateful simply because God *is* the blessing.

Let His love fill you so completely that when you love others, it's not from a place of needing something back. Instead, His love helps you see each person through His eyes and so the most natural thing you do is love them unconditionally.

Worship is bringing the love of God *through the body,* and out into the earth.

It is the beautiful bridge that walks us straight to our purpose which is rejoicing in God.

It brings us directly into sensations, feelings, thoughts that are in unison with Him.

It's where His perfect peace is made manifest *through our hearts.*

What if life was an act of worship?

Your Body, God's Church: Stewarding an Atmosphere of Truth and Growth

The wisest things in life are *invisible*: God, love, breath. These unseen forces shape the tangible world, and they—like an invisible atmosphere—have the power to sustain, protect, and transform.

An atmosphere, by definition, is the pervading tone or mood of a place, situation, or work of art. For Earth, the atmosphere is a jacket of gases that surrounds our planet, providing warmth, oxygen, and a space for weather to take form. Similarly, the atmosphere we carry and cultivate within our bodies is a container that sets the tone for what happens in our lives.

In Genesis 1, in the beginning, we learn that the Spirit of God hovered over a formless void, preparing the atmosphere for creation. On the second day, God separated the waters above from the waters below, placing the sky—an atmosphere—between them. This act of separation was essential; it defined boundaries and created a space where life could flourish.

"Do you not know that your bodies are temples of the Holy Spirit, who is in you, whom you have received from God? You are not your own" (1 Corinthians 6:19).

What we allow into our bodies—physically, mentally, and spiritually—affects the atmosphere we carry and release. Just as Earth's atmosphere determines weather patterns, the atmosphere of your body determines the patterns of your life.

Genesis tells us that the *only* thing separating Heaven and earth is an atmosphere. Meaning, *your body is an atmosphere*. Let that truth sink in: your body is not a mere physical creation; your body, when fully submitted to God, is where Heaven meets earth.

Consider Mary, the mother of Jesus. Her body became the vessel through which the Savior of the world entered. In Luke 1:38, Mary surrendered her will to God's plan, saying, "I am the Lord's servant," and her willingness transformed her into the meeting point for Heaven and earth. Through her *body*, the church—the body of Christ—was set in motion.

Atmospheres separate, surround, and shift the patterns of our world:

- **Separate**: They define boundaries, creating distinct spaces where things either thrive or decay.
- **Surround**: They encase us with conditions that influence growth, shaping outcomes before anything is visibly altered.
- **Shift**: They either stagnate or propel us forward, dictating what is possible in a given space.

Toxic Atmospheres vs. Growth Atmospheres

Who and what you allow into your atmosphere (body) matters. Every person you grant entry to, is also entering into your relationship with God. Are they bringing you closer to Him or further away?

Fear: An Atmosphere of Paralysis

Fear creates an atmosphere that freezes action. It clouds faith, paralyzing decision-making and breeding hesitation. But fear is not something God removes; instead, He counters it with His promise. Fear asks, "What if?" Faith answers, "*Even* if, God is with me." Often, it's not a fear of lack that holds us back, but a fear of becoming the person who can handle the blessing. Will you rise to the occasion, or will fear define your atmosphere?

Comparison: An Atmosphere of Discontent

Comparison distorts reality, creating an atmosphere filled with envy, inadequacy, and striving. To compare is to examine the difference between two or more things, but rarely do we do so to celebrate the things we're examining. Instead, comparison infiltrates perception, leaving us distracted from our unique assignment and blind to God's provision in our lives.

An atmosphere of comparison stunts gratitude and shifts focus from legacy-building to self-pity. Gratitude, on the other hand, anchors you in what God is already doing, providing an opportunity for you to be a trusted steward of more.

Pride: An Atmosphere of Isolation

Pride isolates. It blinds us to wisdom, leading to stagnation and disconnection from God's guidance. Pride says, "I don't need help," and dismisses new beginnings or lessons as beneath us. It fuels the illusion of self-made success, creating a space where true fulfillment becomes impossible.

Scripture warns us: "God opposes the proud but gives grace to the humble" (James 4:6). The antidote to pride is humility, which fosters connection and invites wisdom.

Forget mindset for a moment—ask yourself this: *What kind of atmosphere is my body hosting right now?* Are you hosting fear, pride, or rebellion? Or are you hosting the Spirit of God, releasing truth, peace, and wisdom?

Your Body is the Church

Scripture reminds us that the church is not merely a building; it is the people, the *body* of Christ. God uses human bodies to carry out His Truth and establish His Kingdom. And if your body is a temple of the Holy Spirit, then your body is also a church. It is the dwelling place of God's Spirit, the sacred meeting point between Heaven and earth.

In the same way the early church gathered to strengthen and encourage one another, your body—your church—is called to steward growth, faith, and alignment with God's Will. To host the Holy Spirit is to create an atmosphere where not only you thrive but others are drawn closer to God. Let your body, your church, be a way of light in a world longing for Truth.

God leads. Body calibrates. Mind follows.

What kind of church is your body right now? Is it a sanctuary of the Most High God, or is it weighed down by fear, pride, and rebellion?

Reflect, recalibrate, and invite the Holy Spirit to transform your *atmosphere* and watch everything else follow suit.

Romans 12:1: *"Therefore, I urge you, brothers and sisters, in view of God's mercy, to offer your bodies as a living sacrifice, holy and pleasing to God—this is your true and proper worship."*

John 15:5: *"I am the vine; you are the branches. If you remain in me and I in you, you will bear much fruit; apart from me you can do nothing."*

The Woman of Immovable Faith

There's something undeniable about a woman who walks in the knowing that God *chose* her.

There's something about the way she *speaks*—words wrapped in grace, confidence, and truth. She doesn't need to shout to be heard; her presence speaks louder than a chorus of voices.

There's something about the way she *moves*—with purpose, clarity, and a divine rhythm that can't be disrupted. Her steps are intentional, even in seasons of waiting.

There's something about the way she *drives* her vision forward—not from striving and forcing, but from surrender. She knows her vision isn't her own; it's God's, and because of that, it's unstoppable.

This woman doesn't get taken down by the storms of life. She rests in His grace, knowing the trials are not punishments, but preparation for the journey that lies ahead.

Her immovable faith fulfills her in ways the world never could. She doesn't chase fleeting pleasures or validation; she abides in the love of the One who called her.

And *that* woman?

Her energy is *different.* It's not boastful, and it's not loud. It's a soft confidence that radiates peace and purpose. It's a *steady* assurance. She's exactly where she needs to be, doing exactly what she was created to do.

When she speaks, wisdom flows like a river. When she moves, grace leads the way. When she loves, it's from the overflow of God's love within her.

This woman doesn't just believe in a god; she believes in the Most High God. She believes His promises, His timing, and His purpose for her life.

And because of that, she's unshakable.

Her energy shifts rooms. Because the Spirit of the Living God is within her and she will not fall.

This is the kind of woman the world can't explain, and it's because she's not of the world. She's set apart, chosen, and called.

That woman? She knows who she is because she knows the Almighty God who created her.

Drawing Near to God

God,

Don't move the mountain. *Move me.*

In this moment, I draw near to You.

Make me into Your offering.
Turn me into who You would have me be.

Through my trust in You,
I walk by faith, not by sight.

God, I *put down all my defenses*, all my armor.

I allow Your strength to meet me in my weakness and flaws.
I surrender the cracks that only You can fill.

I *relax my shoulders.*
I lift my chin up towards the sky.
And I remember who You are.

You are the wayshower.
You are the miracle worker.
You are the Holy One.
You are the beginning and the end.
You are the Alpha and the Omega.
You are the God of the universe and You made me for You.

As I walk today, may I remember that You are the one who establishes my steps.
And that You've been here all along.

Lord, in You, I have *everything* I need.
And through You, I will be *everything* I'm designed to be.

Holy Spirit, fill the room.
Guide the way.
Breathe on this day with Truth.

I am listening. I am forever Yours.

And I am so, so grateful to be alive.

In Jesus' Mighty Name,

Amen

About the Author

Victoria Washington is an Entrepreneur, Author, and Speaker leading a financial revolution rooted in faith. As the founder of The House of Wealth Embodiment®, a global faith-based money movement, she empowers trailblazing women of God to create six-figure legacies and beyond through biblical wealth principles.

Her online courses, buzzing membership, and live events break industry standards and pioneer a bridge between faith, finance, and business. With over 10,000 lives impacted, she inspires breakthrough and generational healing one woman and one lineage at a time.

Outside of her work, Victoria cherishes her relationship with Jesus, values family deeply, and enjoys the little things—like perfecting her favorite faux coffee recipe.

Follow VW on Instagram at @iamvictoriawashington/@thehouseofwe.

Join the Holy Yes Movement on Instagram at @theholyyes.

Acknowledgements

**The work that scares you
to teach is delivered by a King
worth being brave for.**

I remember taking a road trip to British Columbia in 2023 to finish the original book I was writing before this one came to life. It was a money book. While eating at a little cafe in Tofino, half writing and half eating, I felt God stop me. This wasn't the book I was meant to be working on.

Jolted by the sudden unexpected awareness, I paused all writing for the rest of the week and simply *listened*. God informed me I would be writing a devotional and that I was to call it *Holy Yes*.

What?

This was the most intimidating news; I quickly questioned if I was ready or if my community was ready. This would be a *major pivot* in a completely different direction than the one I thought I was on.

At the time, I was consulting a psychic for every decision, and still trying to incorporate Jesus into the mix of practices I was still spiritually connected to. This psychic told me to continue writing the original book and that afterwards, *Holy Yes* would be written. Something in that didn't sit right with me. I heard what God said so clearly at the cafe. In that moment, I realized I needed to stop questioning Him and mixing His guidance, with humans who couldn't see His full plan.

When I returned from the trip, I told my editor we were scrapping the original book (for now!) and writing a devotional. She happily jumped on board and we were off.

This book took an avalanche of faith to write, bringing me to my knees in prayer multiple times. Many evenings, my writing turned into worship, each page deepening my love for my Heavenly Father. I didn't know it, but God knew that the process of writing this book would bring me closer to Him than any other work I'd ever create. It would sharpen my discernment, bring me eye to eye with God's Word, and require me to spiritually mature in ways I couldn't have ever prepared for.

Stewarding this book is the greatest honor of my life. And before I publish it, I know in the depths of my heart that all that matters is that He sees it. It's all for Him. *Have Your way, Lord.*

Thank you to Karishma, my editor and companion in writing this book. I'll never forget the day I DM'd you on a whim to see if you'd like to work together. Three years later and you've been the doula I didn't know I needed to bring this book to life. Your tenacity, sharp eye, and brutal honesty were the core qualities God knew I would lean on as I took each step along the way. You are truly one of the most special people I've met in my entire life, and I will cherish this chapter of wrestling on pages to find the right words to bring Him Glory. Thank you.

Thank you to my team, Stephanie Cabey and Justine Mekler. Both of you played a crucial role in creatively bringing this book to life with me. Not one hour, one minute, or one second has gone unnoticed and I'm forever grateful for your continued *Holy Yes*, no matter how wild the ride. I love you and cherish you deeply.

Thank you to my sister, Veronica. Life is crazy isn't it? If only we could have recorded the hundreds of phone conversations we've had over the past two years, many of which shaped the pieces in this book. The way God has us minister to each other never ceases to amaze me. His Spirit is so clearly in you and I'm extremely lucky to have a front row seat to your transformation. Your continued prayers and encouragement to stand ten toes down in faith on the days when I wanted to turn back will never be forgotten. You patiently sat with me while I wrestled with my own will, and let go of other projects before I was ready. In moments of doubt, you reminded me how important this book is, time and time again. God knew I needed you – and I'm so grateful for our sisterhood, friendship, and fellowship.

Thank you to Caroline for shooting the perfect cover. I remember God guiding me to your page and I heard the Holy Spirit say you'd shoot the cover for the book. Just days later we were in a field in Malibu, talking about the Gospel and shooting what would become the cover of *Holy Yes*.

Thank you to Josh Pruitt, video editor extraordinaire. For finding the perfect spot in the Colorado mountains to shoot the first creative videos for the book. You captured the vision so beautifully and I'll always remember that evening on the mountain, complete with pizza and belly laughs at the end of a long day.

And last but certainly not least, to my community. I love each of you so, so much. Every testimony, every DM, every story you've shared with me about your walk with Christ was divinely timed by God and encouraged me to finish this book. On the days where I couldn't find the words, I thought of you. The truth is, you believed in this book before I ever did. And for that, I'm eternally grateful.

To my precious Lord and Savior Jesus, thank You for the ride of a lifetime. I pray Your daughters flock to Your feet and rest in Your ever-lasting love. I will minister Your Gospel as long as You allow me to.

Resources

Bible Recommendation:
- While there are many versions of the Bible, the one I recommend is the *NIV Artisan Collection Bible* or *CSB Christian Standard Bible.*

Starting Your Journey with Christ:
- *Holier Than Thou: How God's Holiness Helps Us Trust Him* by Jackie Hill Perry
- *Mere Christianity* by C. S. Lewis (really, anything by C.S Lewis)

Daily Grace and Guidance:
- *Seamless: Understanding the Bible as One Complete Story* by Angie Smith
- *The Knowledge of the Holy: The Attributes of God* by A. W. Tozer
- *Upon Waking: 60 Daily Reflections to Discover Ourselves and the God We Were Made For* by Jackie Hill Perry

Living a Christ-Centered Life
- *Are You Praying for the Wrong Thing?: Learning to Ask What God Wants for You, Not Just What You Want* by Travis Greene
- *Leadership as an Identity: The Four Traits of Those Who Wield Lasting Influence* by Crawford W. Loritts
- *Single, Dating, Engaged, Married: Navigating Life and Love in the Modern Age* by Ben Stuart
- *The Maxwell Leadership Bible* by Thomas Nelson
- *Welcome to the Basement: An Upside-Down Guide to Greatness Hardcover* by Tim Ross
- *Woman Evolve: Break Up with Your Fears and Revolutionize Your Life* by Sarah Jakes Roberts

Going Deeper with God
- *The Awe of God: The Astounding Way a Healthy Fear of God Transforms Your Life* by John Bevere

- *The Person of Christ (Contours of Christian Theology)* by Donald Macleod
- *The Showings of Julian of Norwich: A New Translation* by Mirabai Starr